Who's Killing the Church?

a renewal reader

EDITED BY STEPHEN C. ROSE

SELECTIONS BY DON BENEDICT, L. K. BISHOP, GORDON COSBY, HARVEY COX, JOHN FRY, BRUCE HUNT, HOWARD MOODY, JARED RARDIN, ROBERT SPIKE, BILL SOUTHWICK, ROBERT STROM, AND PEGGY WAY

IN memory of James Reeb, Jonathan Daniels, Viola Liuzzo, Jimmie Lee Jackson, William Moore, Medgar Evers, James Chaney, Andrew Goodman, Mickey Schwerner, the children of Birmingham and all others who, wittingly or not, have taken upon themselves the crucifixions of our time.

a renewal reader/$1.50

"Who's Killing The Church?" A Renewal Reader
Copyright © 1966 by the Chicago City Missionary Society
Published by
Renewal Magazine   Association Press
19 South La Salle Street 291 Broadway
Chicago, Illinois 60603   New York, N. Y. 10007

Manufactured in the United States of America
All rights reserved

Contents

Introduction : : 4

Part One: A Crisis of Definition : : 7
    "I've Been Asked to Leave My Church" : : 8
    A New Freedom for Ministry : : 13
    What's Wrong with The Church: The Clergy : : 20
    The Pit Between The Pulpit And The Pew : : 24
    Women in The Church: Comic Strip, Society Section or Front Page? : : 30

Part Two: Does The Church Need A New Structure? : : 41
    Structures for The New Era : : 42
    Into The World of Work : : 49
    Not Renewal, but Reformation : : 53
    The Denominational Dollar : : 59

Part Three: Does The Local Church Have A Future? : : 69
    Sainthood Before Strategy : : 70
    Study And Faith in Suburbia : : 77
    Toward A Religionless Church for A Secular World : : 82

Part Four: Needed: An Approach to The Future : : 93
    Saying Yes To Leisure : : 94
    The Uses of Leisure Time : : 102
    Experiment: Chicago's Door : : 105
    Freedom Now! : : 108
    Apathy, Abdication and Acedia : : 110

Part Five: Postscripts, Biases and Sundry Observations : : 117
    Whither The Gospel in Race Relations? : : 118
    The Post-Assassination Church : : 124

INTRODUCTION

WHO'S killing the Church? An explanation of our title is in order. In recent years, observers in and out of the churches have spoken of a general decline in religious interest. Man, they say, has become secularized. He no longer needs the props of faith and he is losing interest in the institutional expression of religion, the Church. In Europe the churches are practically empty and in the United States there is a gradual decline in membership, particularly in large metropolitan areas. From this perspective, the Church is dying because modern man is either too apathetic or too self-sufficient to involve himself in the life of the religious establishment. Who's killing the Church? Modern man who, contrary to the late Professor Jung, is no longer in search of a soul. His accomplices are the depersonalized modern metropolis, the sweep of contemporary technology, and the general lack of concern for one's fellow man that these forces seem to produce.

There are some, however, who feel this analysis is too simple. It does not take sufficient notice of the Church's own shortcomings. Who's killing the Church? Don't blame the world, says this second group, because the real crime against the Church is being committed from within. The Church is being killed by her own failure to take the shape that the world needs. If the Church were being murdered by villains from the outside, if it were facing persecution for its witness in the world, there might be hope. But the world doesn't persecute a Church that seems to stand for nothing. So the verdict is more serious: suicide, a slow death resulting from what Arnold Toynbee has called a "failure of nerve."

There is a third interpretation which grows out of the second. It recognizes that the Church today is in ferment. Some are feverishly trying to maintain the status quo—the emphasis on expensive buildings, on wishy-washy moralizing that masquerades as preaching, on studious efforts to involve laymen in trivial tasks rather than honest confrontation with the demands of the Gospel. But others are sensing a new spirit in the wind, a spirit which is calling the Church to lay down its life for the world. The spirit has moved Christians into the heart of the fight for justice in our society; it has begun to replace inconsequential church work with a renewed wrestling with the

INTRODUCTION ::5

deep implications of Christian faith. It blows through traditional parishes and gives birth to experimental ministries, whether in the bars of Chicago, the slums of New York, or the leisure spots of Las Vegas. There are some who feel that this is the spirit of God—whether expressed in the vision of a Pope John XXIII or in the martyrdom of ministers and laymen in the deep South—and that this spirit is calling for the death of the Church as we know it. Who's killing the Church? God Himself. The Church is called to lose her life in order to find new life.

The writers of this book are convinced that the impending death of the Church cannot be blamed on outside forces. They look to the signs of death within the churches. Some of the signs are seen as emblems of suicide and disobedience. Others are seen as the working out of a new consciousness, a new spirit, within the very fabric of the Church. Thus we offer a series of manifestoes, suggestions and observations—all of them designed to call forth within the religious establishment a vast outpouring of conscious dedication both to the present word of God and to the task of servanthood in the world. This is a call for a renewal movement within Protestantism, a movement that will join forces with progressive fellow Christians of Orthodox and Roman Catholic backgrounds, and begin to write a new page of Church history, a page that will read: "For the first time since the Reformation, Christians were brought together not merely on the basis of creeds and doctrine, but because they heard the voice of one God calling them to work together in the streets and alleys, factories and offices, hospitals and legislative offices of a world in need of sacrificial service and dedicated commitment."

What follows is the work of many persons, but it is one book. Its five sections are designed to raise specific issues which must be dealt with by clergymen, laymen and Church officials if significant renewal is to take place. It is hoped that the chapters will be studied individually and as a whole throughout the Church, not only Protestant but Roman Catholic and Orthodox as well—so that a common language of concern for our faith and for the world will develop. What is presented is not definitive, but suggestive. But there is enough that is precise and definite to offer to any reader or church study group a plan of action and a vision of what must begin to take place throughout the religious community.

With one exception, the following selections all appeared in recent issues of *Renewal Magazine,* a publication sponsored jointly by the Chicago City Missionary Society and the New York City Mission Society. We have undertaken the publication of this book as an experiment. If response warrants it, we shall from time to time, present additional volumes designed to serve as a continued catalyst for renewal in the Church. This book is aimed primarily at laymen, although we hope that ministers, denominational officials and seminary students will find it useful. Our conviction is that a renewed laity is the key factor in the renewal of the Church. In one sense the Church will never die because there will always remain a core of faithful witnesses to the action and love of God in Christ. But if the Church as it exists today is to be reborn, the constructive alterations suggested in the following pages may prove to be at least a midwife in the difficult process of change. ☐

PART ONE
A CRISIS OF DEFINITION

The five articles that follow all raise a single insistent question: How are we to understand the mission of the Church in our time? Is the Church merely a "bland island of serenity" or is it meant to be a vanguard of God's people carrying Christ's word of love and justice into the controversial corners of the world? If it is the latter, can we continue to exist with our present definitions of the roles of clergy and laity? Can we bridge the widening gap between the pulpit and the pew? Can the current activities within the Church building be regarded as a worthwhile substitute for active engagement in the world? The suggestion of the writers is that the Church will continue to fade away unless ministers and laymen sit down together to hammer out these issues. From such debate there might emerge a new and vital definition of the Church and its mission. □

"I've Been Asked to Leave My Church"

—Anonymous

I'VE been asked to leave my church. Time was when that line, spoken by a minister, was a very dramatic one, like the line in so many movies during the depression, in which the father of the household comes bursting through the doorway, holds his head, and exclaims, "I've been wiped out!" Both lines are almost cliches, now. The only excuse for discussing the situation of the minister who is asked to leave is just that it is so common.

I am pastor of a church of over a thousand members in the suburban area that surrounds a large city in three states. Most of the breadwinners among the members of this church have their work in this city. They are bankers, brokers, merchants, attorneys, business men of all kinds. I don't think that the fact that this is a "big church" or a "suburban church" has very much to do with the situation. Time and again, I have thought how much this church reacts like country churches of about a hundred members. When I was pastor of such a country church, I thought the provincialism I occasionally encountered must be attributable to the rural mode of thought. Now I know that, in church, Wall Street and Rural Route 36 think very much alike. One finds the same kindness, thoughtfulness, and wisdom, the same smallness and ignorance, in all places.

One day in December I came into the church office—I had just been out to mail a letter—and another member of the church staff grasped at this moment to have a "heart to heart talk" with me. It was his judgment that I ought to look for another pastorate. "Things are in terrible shape! People are coming to me all the time to complain about your work!" This young man was employed to assist me, and he was doing the right thing to report to me his impressions. A layman, he was serving in an administrative capacity in the church office. His approach to the problem was awkward, but sincere, I was sure. Ironically, the letter I had just mailed was a response to a query another church had made about the availability of my services. It is probably an illustration of my naivete that I had replied that I wasn't interested. "I hope to have a long pastorate where I am," I had said.

I talked with the young man in the church office and I talked with some of my Elders. I couldn't discover what the specific complaints were. For several months I had been the sole minister on the church staff, my associate having left early in the fall to become pastor of another church. The volume of work was getting me down, but I was confident that the church people would be patient about my inability to carry a double load as effectively as two men could do.

Things happened rapidly. I consulted the Presbytery Committee on Ministerial Relations, and I consulted with more of my Elders. There was a special session meeting from which I was absent, in which the body unanimously passed a "vote of confidence." The wording, I thought, was rather guarded and bland, but I attributed that quality to the grammar and the rhetoric of the business world, and I took it at face value. The minister who had agreed to come as my associate wisely backed out when he heard of the little skirmish we were having. "I'm interested in working with *you*," he said, "and this difficulty in your church may yet result in your leaving." So, I was without staff assistance for some months more.

Things went along reasonably well until May. There had been an uncommon amount of illness and other personal tragedy among the church people, so that the pastoral load was great. Lent and Easter were difficult because of the extra services and meetings that they added, with which I had previously had assistance. I thought I could take a break after Easter, but that was impossible because of the pastoral needs in the parish. I was making a hundred calls a month, and working with the session's committee to seek another staff minister. We found a young man of great promise, and he agreed to come. This time there seemed to be no hitch, for the "vote of confidence" was now a matter of record, and now there could be a sincere effort to develop a program to make the pastoral relationship more effective. We were fully staffed again, or would be very soon.

The evening before the session was to meet our young prospective assistant for his first interview, I was asked to meet with two of the Elders of the church. I met them by appointment in my study, and one of them opened the conversation by offering prayer. This was sufficiently unusual to be indicative of his embarrassment, I thought. After the prayer, the spokesman said "Perhaps you have some idea why we wanted to talk to you?" "Yes." And then I told them of the lines from a television drama that had been written by a friend of mine. The minister looks out his living room window on Sunday afternoon and sees three men of his church coming up to his door. He receives them, and one says "I suppose you wonder why we've come, Pastor? The minister replies, "Yes, when people are in trouble they come alone, but when they come in three's, *I'm* in trouble!"

There was an embarrassed silence. Then the Elder who had spoken spoke again. He explained his deep appreciation for my talents, and he assured me that nobody had any complaints about my preaching, but it seemed to him and to some others that my unusual talents would be most useful somewhere else, where undoubtedly I could be a very successful minister. The spokesman, it turned out later, had authored the "vote of confidence." It had been a fraudulent expression of faith, a mere bid for time, a device to keep the pastor silent.

Still, there was no hint of "The Trouble." Was there suspicion that I was a secret alcoholic? Had I been accused of some gross impropriety? None of these. It was—well, just that *this* pastor and *this* parish didn't seem to fit each other.

"Why?" I said, unwilling to let go.

"Well," said the more talkative Elder, "if it's one thing more than anything else, it's that we get the idea that you're trying to *change* us." I couldn't suppress a smile as I said "Yes?"

That was the point at which the talk really broke down. The Elder had said what he hadn't intended to say . . . that he wanted a gospel that didn't try to change him. There wasn't much to be said after that, except that "for your own good" they hoped I'd give consideration to seeking quietly another pastorate. It was understood that if I didn't see it that way, they would have to bring it up in a session meeting.

I told them that I'd think it over, but I also said that I thought them wrong on at least two counts. First, I didn't think the disaffection with my ministry was so general as it seemed to them. Second, I said I thought the discomfort they were feeling was not due to any unseemly effort on my part to change them. There is, I said, a growing tension between the church and the world, and we feel admonished and condemned when we encounter the church. "We assume, then, that there is something wrong with the church," I said. "The fact is, there'd be something wrong with the church if we *didn't* feel it! You know that our state, our town, our neighborhoods tolerate some things that the church has to oppose. Feeling that tension, you feel that someone must be nagging you."

I realized what the real trouble was. A few weeks before, most of the clergymen in town—all of the Roman Catholics and about 80% of the Protestants—had signed a statement and published it in the local paper, advocating the end of racially restricted housing in our community. A few weeks before that, I had preached a sermon on the subject of race relations, my first in over a year. Well, I certainly wasn't the first minister to be asked to leave because of that interpretation of the Gospel. My lot is much easier than that of the ousted ministers in the South who are threatened with anonymous telephone calls, whose parishioners cut off their credit and turn the whole community against them.

In one small way, however, my situation was more difficult. No one will admit that the race issue has anything to do with the problem. The reasons given by those who are whispering about the parish that I am "looking for another job" are that I don't remember names (of the whole thousand members and their families), that I don't dress neatly enough, that I don't call enough, that I spend too much time on Presbytery work, that the children's sermons I used to have in the services (up until two years ago) weren't dignified, that my wife shouldn't be employed (with three children in college at once, and aging parents to help support).

Fortunately, the courageous young man who was considering the staff position as my assistant agreed to come, even when I joined with Presbytery's Ministerial Relations Committee to tell him about the situation.

Friends and supporters are urging me to stay on. They tell me sincerely, "The church needs a pastor who will face issues as you do." "It isn't right to let a dissident handful of people control the policies of the church!" "You must stay and fight it out!" Perhaps I will have made the point if I leave and let the real leaders of the church discover that they have to express their leadership more positively if the church is to stand for anything more than the status quo. Perhaps my ministry here is now stultified by the very fact that a shadow has been cast on my effectiveness because questions were raised about it.

Yet I am hounded and haunted by the implication that if I leave I am saying that no church is really a Church, but a bland island of serenity for people who agree in all things. Let us imagine that any pastor, the Rev. Mr. X, comes to any church. Some faction of the congregation will find the pastor's theology, program, social views, and wife acceptable. Others, perhaps a very minor fraction, will not like his theology, his program, his social views, or his wife. The way things are pointing, it seems that ultimately the latter group is bound to find a spokesman who will have the courage or the temerity to approach the pastor and ask him to leave. Their efforts won't stop there, however, and at last the minister will begin to wonder if he hasn't stayed out his usefulness to that parish.

The minister is no longer a person—or parson—set apart from his people, except symbolically by the ordination ceremony. The lay members of the church aren't afraid of him, cowed by him, or even awed by his learning. All of this is good, but like the side effects of some modern wonder drugs, there are problems that attend the new comradeship between clergy and laity. The Ministerial Relations Committee of our Presbytery is very reluctant to reveal anything about their confidential counselling of pastors, sessions, and congregations, but when I asked the chairman if their work had increased in the past ten years, he replied that it had increased a thousand percent in *two* years. This probably means that half the churches in our presbytery are having "trouble with the minister."

The demands of the Christian Faith will sometimes be in conflict with the values of society. If this ferment in the churches means that the people are discovering that the conflict exists, that is good. If it means that they are trying to find ways to surrender, so that the conflict is avoided, then may God help the church! ☐

A New Freedom for Ministry

By Robert C. Strom

THE profession of clergyman is becoming an impossible burden for anyone needing a sense of meaningful vocation. Demands for a clerical class to maintain religious institutions are now being rejected. Seminary enrollment drops year by year. Religious bodies frantically search for clergy recruits. Vacant pulpits multiply. Countless ministers seek some sense of authentic vocation through frenzied activism or perpetual contemplation of ecclesiastical navels. We are observing the death throes of the professional ministry. A way must be suggested to hasten the demise and to free at once those bound by a languishing clericalism.

I am a kinsman of today's ministers, and my lifelong lot is cast with them. I am a graduate of a denominational seminary, an ordained minister in a protestant denomination, and have served seven years in parish churches. It is this personal involvement which compels me to diagnose the cleric's vocation as a terminal illness and to suggest some tentative steps toward a new freedom for ministry.

The initial recognition of clerical sickness may be traced to the Reformation. At that moment in history there emerged the first widespread awareness since before Constantine that the primary concern of Christians is not with the religious establishment but with the world. Medieval Christendom placed church in authority over the world, giving the professional representatives of the church an organic and legitimate function in society.

The Reformers proclaimed that the world in all its diversity is redeemed by Christ and that the function of the church is not to seek dominion over that world, but to exist in the world as one servant among many witnessing to the activity of God.

This should have changed the location of ministry from the religious enclosure to the market place. But vested interest and centuries of tradition prevented this change from taking root. Protestantism could not see far enough to let the church die as an institution set against the world. Thus the clergy was perpetuated as a class existing to maintain the establishment.

Ministers were ordained to function in a sterile structure with no authentic relation to the world.

Today we are at last realizing the radical implications of the revolution against the Christendom of the Middle Ages. The complexity of a new society emerging under the impact of urbanization can be understood as God at work pushing us to realize that the church has no ministry if it lacks genuine involvement in the world. We are being forced to understand that it is totally false to place church against world. There is only one reality—the world. And we are all a part of that God-given and God-sustained reality. There is one holy place—the world. Holy worldliness is the stance of Christianity.

There is no justification for the ordination of a class of priests separated from the world. Preaching of the Word and breaking of bread are necessary in the Christian life. But preaching need not take place behind church walls, and bread can be broken by other than professionals. The gospel is not for the holy enclave but for the crossroads of culture. The sickness of the clergy today is that the entire milieu—the authentic context—of the professional ministry has been lost. Ministers have no professional identity because they exist in a world of unreality. No matter how much we try to convince ourselves that there is a special validity to the religious enterprise, we cannot forget that Christ came *to* the world, died *for* the world, and that his followers were witnesses to his resurrection *in* the world.

The residentially-based parish church is where the vast majority of today's clergymen are to be found. The other day I passed the bulletin board of such a church displaying a poster-picture of a mountain. The days of the week were camps on the slope. Monday was at the base, Tuesday a little higher, then Wednesday, Thursday, Friday, Saturday. The summit was Sunday, with the caption: "Your high point—good preaching, good music, friendly neighbors." Sunday at this suburban establishment was portrayed as the pinnacle of weekly experience by a clergyman whose religious product symbolized retreat from the complex life of the world.

The minister, insecure in his vocational identity, often attempts conforming to traditional clergy roles in establishing his place in society. Such attempts are sure to fail.

For example, Sunday worship was once a "high point" of the week for those who might expect to hear the prophetic word. Today the authentic role of clergyman as *prophet* has degenerated. The prophet must be aware of God's activity in the world and then speak of this activity to the religious community. An urbanized world requires full-time attention if there is to be prophetic discernment. Institutional demands of the parish church compel the minister to stand aloof from the market place, observe its activities through the mirrors of religiosity and then pretend to be spokesman for God. The clergyman seeking true prophetic involvement in today's society will threaten his ordained status through neglect of his clerical duties.

Ministerial efforts to be *shepherd of the flock* are also doomed. There is no valid basis upon which the flock is gathered today. We cannot expect men to be called out of the world in which they live and group themselves on a spiritual basis. The foundation of the residential congregation was that members lived closely together from economic and social necessity. The local congregation was once a functional unit of a primary community. Now citizens of the metropolis find such basic community in vocational, professional, political and economic spheres beyond the community of residence. Yet the clergyman still addresses a ministry to "his parish," vainly trying to call the sheep together. There is nothing more pathetic than a shepherd treading well-worn paths to call sheep that are not there. A minister peddling spiritual values out of context with human community is a parasite. It is not that the sheep need no shepherd. It is that the shepherd is deprived of his flock by trying to maintain his traditional role rather than dropping the shepherd's crook and robe and donning the contemporary dress of a man involved in the world as it is.

Another symbolic role of the professional clergy is demolished as the average cleric attempts to be a *burden bearer* for his people. He may try to lift the weights from bent shoulders, but finds that, although he can occasionally patch the raw skin, he cannot shoulder the burdens. He is cut off from the source of the problems that are piled on the backs of men and women today. There was a time when such burdens were primarily spiritual and when the confessional function of the ordained priest was a necessity. But as man has come of age seeking wholeness of life, he has been unable to separate the religious from the political, social and economic. His burdens are one. There is no place for a man with the special task of bearing spiritual burdens.

We are entering the time when the church must be the community of laymen called out by Christ to bear one another's burdens and not to carry those heavy weights to a priesthood set apart from life. The only way to reestablish the function of burden bearer in the church is for the minister to divest himself of his priestly illusions, and join the company of laymen in the world who are weighted and bruised and broken together by the problems of modern metropolitan society and then made whole together in a common ministry.

Consider finally the ancient role of clergyman as *father*. Each time I have donned the clerical collar to officially represent the church in today's society, I have been addressed by many as "father." But I cannot ignore the smirk of some who hear me called father. They realize any organic relationship I may have had to society as a family is gone. And thus any authority as a father in the family has been destroyed. In the new world that is coming to be, the clergyman can no longer expect to be the authority father figure. We need have no theological debates about authority. Except in our religious fantasy there is no clerical authority. A culture which demands vocations of participation in social and economic processes places no authority in a non-functional clerical order. Men as they come of age refute the influence of a man who claims to be father by virtue of divine right. Fatherhood is a privilege given only to those who declare their oneness with the human family.

In the face of such disturbing evaluation of the ministry today, what alternatives are open for the future? There seem to be only two. Men can continue to dedicate themselves to the ordained clergy and to exist in the illusory world of the religious institution, convincing themselves that we can return to the Christendom of the Middle Ages. Such a dedication can be satisfying for

—those who need illusion to appear larger than life.

—those who believe God is confined to the religious institution.

—those who are convinced that an urbanized world is demonic and choose detachment from its taint.
—those who affirm that Christ was divine spirit, but not fully human.

But for those who reject such false satisfaction, there can only be faith that today's laymen and clergymen will face the plain fact that there is no need for an ordained professional ministry.

In seeking new freedom for ministry, the first step is to uproot clericalism by exposing it as a sickness and recognizing the bondage of illusion which it creates. Beyond this expose, there must be a suggestion of outlines for a future ministry. These suggestions emerge from the understanding of Christian ministry as function rather than clerical class. The function of ministry in the primitive church was servanthood in the world. The equipment of the saints for ministry was a preparation for service. Today the church must rediscover what it means to witness to its Servant Lord in the midst of the world.

A first realistic step away from clericalism will be the willingness of denominations to foster *experimental ministries*. Models of new ministries are needed to conquer fear of losing the economic base of operation provided by the residential parish. Churches and clergymen will refuse to scrap traditional programs without some clear idea of what the future might hold. Our major denominations must begin to invest significant sums in ministries which could point the way to the forms of the future.

Attacks on the traditional ministerial role are not unusual today. There are widespread signs of dissatisfaction among clergymen. The Spirit is speaking to the church today through this kind of dissatisfaction. It is up to the denominations with the greatest financial resources to encourage unfulfilled clergymen to move out from one traditional role to a variety of experiments. Let the church encourage men to develop new and diverse forms by giving them realistic financial support. Such action will involve risks. Denominational boards and agencies cannot expect a sure return on experimental investments. But the church will lose life to find it in diverting funds from copying old and sterile forms of ministry. Search for new forms of the servant church in the world will proclaim the relevance of the gospel to a changing culture. In church extension, for example, the budget is usually given to fabricating copies of established religious institutions. Can we continue to be satisfied with this limited definition of church extension? Should we not initiate experiments free from statistical expectations for buildings, budget and specific program, entering not only the high potential suburbs, but also the inner city, to listen to what's happening in the world and then to allow the ministry to grow from the situation?

Another possible experimental form is the cell-group structured around specific issues requiring study and action. The lay apostolate needs to be called out from the residential community of conformity to a ministry of reading the signs of the times, and pointing to new forms of service in such areas as public education, housing, welfare business and industry. Use of mission funds for such experiments would free clergymen from playing a role, to a new sense of vocation. Theologically and biblically trained pastors could become the charismatic catalysts for countless new forms of ministry.

Moving further beyond clericalism will require *functional ordination*. We now ordain divinity graduates to the "office of the Holy Ministry." What does this mean if ministry belongs to the laity, the whole people of God? It implies that our lack of functionally defined ordination is an intentional continuation of a clerical class. We have gone beyond the definition of church as the holy place where the word is preached and the sacraments administered. Word and sacraments must be understood in relation to specific areas of involvement in the world. Refusal to ordain a man without a precise definition of intended ministry would be in the spirit of the New Testament which is very specific about defining the function of church members:

"Now you are the body of Christ and individually members of it, and God has appointed in the church first apostles, second prophets, third teachers, then workers of miracles, then healers, helpers, administrators, speakers in various kinds of tongues." (I Cor. 12:27, 28).

Let our denominations move beyond theoretical study of the nature of the ministry, and put into practice the growing awareness that theological training should be in the context of ministry in industry, ministry in politics, ministry in law, etc.

A third practical step toward erasing a clerical vocation would follow functional ordination. If all Christians are ordained to some ministry at baptism, and if then further special ordination is required only in functional recognition of responsibility, such ordination should be extended to laymen. The focus of a new freedom for ministry would be the *training of the laity* for ministry. Seminaries, free from the necessity of maintaining a clerical class, could become centers for equipping the laity for their vocation in the world.

Seminary curriculums gutted of courses in sacerdotal techniques and theological, biblical and liturgical obscurities could begin to add one and two-year training courses for men in science, business, industry, politics, medicine, and law. This training would point the way toward the functions of teaching and preaching and healing and the sacraments being given to the laity, as well as encouraging lay ministry within vocation. Money for such programs could be obtained not only from denominational sources but also from foundations interested in new levels of excellence in business, politics, social welfare and education.

Training for ministry should also move beyond established theological seminaries. One such endeavor is the Urban Training Center in Chicago. It is an interdenominational effort to train students for a mission to the metropolis. Residentially-based parishes could also become lay training centers.

These are but first steps in a search for new freedom for ministry. The search must begin. Let clericalism be uprooted once and for all. A new freedom for ministry is the freedom which belongs to all of us because of Jesus Christ our Lord. It is a freedom to participate fully in the world over which He is Lord. It is the freedom to leave illusion and step into reality as it is in this moment. It is the freedom to choose relevant forms of service rather than outmoded institutional and liturgical sterility. It is a freedom to be as revolutionary in our vocation as is our Lord risen and in our midst. As Dietrich Bonhoeffer has written: "The church is not a religious community of worshippers of Christ, but is Christ Himself who has taken form among men." In the final analysis, the new freedom for ministry will be our freedom to take form as Christ himself among men *as they are* in this moment of history. ☐

What's Wrong With The Church: The Clergy

By Peggy Way

THERE is a popular parlor game played by ministers called "What's Wrong with the Church?" It is somewhat similar to "Pin the Tail on the Donkey." Ministers, in rather dizzy fashion, as if blindfolded, pin their criticisms on the Church which is certainly viewed as a donkey.

Yet the game itself is really not my major concern. It is merely symptomatic of something more basically wrong with the present generation of ministers. For often it seems to me that what is wrong with the church is the clergy—who fail to pin the pointed tails of criticism on themselves, who seek to involve laymen in church programs with which they themselves cannot identify and about which they are cynical, who preach a morality which is not operative in their own lives, who reject the depths of the cross and the meaning of unreserved, compassionate love.

The painful answer to the question, "What is wrong with the church?" is "I, the minister, am what is wrong."

Ministers are concerned and judgmental about the status drives in other professions. But young pastors are quite aware of the appropriate steps upward in their denomination, through the ranks of assistant and associate, to the choice committee assignments.

Putting on the clerical collar for special occasions (including racial demonstrations and visits to traffic court) does not hide the minister's underlying passion for success—for material possessions, for a parsonage (or his own home) that is at least on the level of others in his community, for climbing the ladders that exist within the institution. Laymen and fresh young pastors may not realize that rivalries in the church are not unlike rivalries in the business community, except that in the latter competition is less concealed. We hear representatives of ecumenical groups arguing with denominational officials concerning who speaks for whom, when, how, and with what important secular body. Suburban, inner city, rural pastors, and those engaged in new forms of ministry, vie with each other for position and funds and self-consciously justify their existences to each other.

There is among us a sense of embarrassment at being pastors. More and more we become ashamed of our legitimate pastoral role and less and less challenged by it. More and more we discuss the problems of being a pastor, and less its rare opportunities. Embarrassed and uncertain of where we stand, it is no wonder that we turn elsewhere for our standards, our images of success.

Far too many of our younger clergy (from self-analytical seminarian to bright young denominational executive) are themselves lost souls—proclaiming the Gospel out of emptiness, intellectually brilliant but faulty in personal relationships. Again and again we find the fine young man whose conflicts with his congregation are explained on the level of principle (his being right) rather than on the level of his personal practice and witness to the principle. Sometimes congregations unjustly bear the weight of criticism for not being able to get along with their pastor, when in fact he may lack the personal and professional maturity to know how to make his faith and principles incarnate among them.

The ministry can also become the ideal spot for the person who would speak out on controversial issues without experiencing any genuine risk—the pains of the pocketbook, public rejection, the cross. How many of our civil rights demonstrators demonstrate and are bailed out on an expense account? How many of our younger ministers would move into an unrehabilitated parsonage? How many find glee in momentary martyrdom? How many have sufficient personal resources of faith to stand, at the last moment, alone—feeling not only in others but in themselves the pain of ultimate imperfection, complete failure, the sense of forsakenness experienced by Christ on the cross?

More and more seminarians, pastors, and denominational executives seek out the services of professional psychiatrists, or are referred by fellow pastors or faculty members who feel incompetent to deal with them. Again and again we meet those who have a fine understanding of their symptoms, but only vague feelings for the roots of their discontent.

Most clergymen are agreed that the moral edicts of the Victorian period are inadequate for our day, but in rejecting old moralisms they have found few solid precepts for constructing modern systems of ethics. We have not found appropriate criteria to guide ourselves and others in making moral decisions.

Have we looked deeply enough into the real meaning of the severe marital and sexual crises of our younger clergy? Have we heard the implications of the statement that it may be immoral to remain with a wife that is not loved just because there are children involved in the event of divorce? Have we heard what is said when a married minister finds a real personal relationship and understands himself to be making incarnate the Biblical meaning of "to know one another"—with a woman who is not his wife? Do we even talk together openly about what such pressing personal problems tell us about ourselves, our understanding of the ministry, our understanding of the theologies that guide us?

How can we minister to others when we have not honestly admitted we ministers share the whole gamut of problems faced by all persons? And how, heaven help us, can we share moral standards with others when we have not worked them through for ourselves?

We are selectively compassionate. I feel for this person; for that one, I do not. With this group I can minister; with that group I cannot.

The increasing mobility of ministers tends to prevent deep relationships with the people of any one congregation. The increasing size and complexity of churches tends to fragment our relationships with families and with individuals within the context of their total life situations. Not really knowing our people, we readily judge and stereotype them. If they speak the "wrong" words, we may close our ears to them. If they look like junior executives and suburban housewives, we may no longer see them sitting in our congregations seeking, perhaps in quiet desperation, the Word of God. If we cannot get along with them, we can always move on to another church.

We stereotype one another. He—the historical liberal—has nothing to say. She—the old-maid Christian educator—would rather find a man than teach. He—choosing the town and country ministry—doesn't have the stuff to go where the "real" issues are. She—the seminary student—will never be accepted as a pastor.

We also stereotype the meaning to be found in various forms of worship. We sometimes pride ourselves in not letting our congregations sing the old Gospel hymns. We minimize the importance of the sermon, and choose to put our time elsewhere. We expect our congregations to move immediately into more significant forms of worship, forgetting that they are probably no more adept than we in changing overnight. We stereotype our laymen, our session members, the participants in our ladies' auxiliaries. We forget that not every layman has the privilege of having gone through four years of college and three years of graduate school. We wait for them to ask questions in *our* words, and cannot hear them when they use their own.

We are so busy stereotyping aspects of church life and the persons of our parishioners and our fellow pastors, that we do not hear their questions; we do not touch them where they are living; we do not smell the aroma of rejection that we emit.

It is my contention that this generation of pastors stands in the way of church renewal. But my purpose is not to deny, but to affirm. The renewal of the church is underway at those moments when we look most deeply into ourselves. It is underway when we ministers reach out to the layman, sharing with him all of our failure and self-doubt, our pretentions as well as our passions. Renewal is underway when we ask our congregations not to expect us to be more than we are, but to share with us the task of becoming more than we are through the community we share in common, graced by a God who makes no distinctions between layman and minister.

The renewal of the church demands mutual repentance. We cannot judge others for lacking what we ourselves do not have. Somewhere renewal must have its beginning point. And perhaps that point lies in the willingness of ministers and laymen to sit down together and recognize that the task they face is a common one. Instead of walking to the mourner's wall with his fellow clergymen and despairing of his job, let the minister share his concerns within the congregation of which he is a part. In this age of seeking, let the minister apply the hopeful words of Christ—"Seek and ye shall find"—to both himself and the congregation he is serving. Let the minister restore *his* faith by joining with laymen in the quest for understanding and meaning that is so crucial in our time. □

The Pit Between the Pulpit and the Pew

By Dr. L. K. Bishop

For many years we have recognized the problem of communication between the physician and his patient, between the scientist and the businessman, the industrialist and the government official. We have not been surprised to discover that the social scientist and the physical scientist could not understand each other, but it comes as a shock to discover that the clergyman, whose business it is to counsel with people, to communicate with people, to understand people, is suffering from this modern *disease of specialization*.

Without assessing blame or indicting either layman or clergyman, we must seek to focus sharply on the increasing difficulty of bridging the barriers between the pulpit and the pew.

A vice-president of one of America's largest corporations, active in his own church, writes: "For a long time I have been troubled to note the difficulties the church seems to have in trying to talk to businessmen in their role as businessmen."

A professor in a school of religion picks up the theme and comments: "There is a deep and constantly growing feeling among the Protestant laity of America to the effect that something is missing from the life and message of their churches."

With a plaintive cry a suburban churchman, active in his church work, reflects his own bewilderment when he says: "I've been unable to understand the language ministers use for so long that I no longer can look to professional clergymen for guidance in my faith. Why are ministers so obscure? Why can't they phrase things so laymen can understand?"

Ministers, equally bewildered and obviously conscious of the increasing distance between themselves and their leadership, comment frankly on the problem. One minister asks: "Isn't a part of the problem that people don't feel a need for dogmas, creeds and elaborate phrasing of the gospels? How can you communicate the need for love and for forgiveness to persons who are wealthy enough to wall themselves off from elementary needs? What meaning has the gospel for the self-sufficient?" Another minister, recognizing the barrier between himself and his leadership commented in these terse words: "My church governing board includes a businessman of questionable ethics, a doctor who refused medical attention to one indigent family, and a real estate man who was instrumental in keeping Negroes from buying homes in our suburb."

One businessman, in trying to illustrate the great distance that exists between himself and his clergyman, reported a part of a prayer which his minister had given: "Oh Lord, deliver us from lying, called propaganda, and from plunder, called profits." For this business executive whose life was dedicted to free enterprise and whose existence depended upon profitable business operations, it was inconceivable that his clergyman could look on profits as plunder.

The *Harvard Business Review* reports a survey of 1700 executives who were asked, "How much guidance did your church and clergyman provide for the ethical problems you faced in the last five years?" For those who gave an answer, four out of five were dissatisfied with what the clergy had done for them. Twenty percent indicated the church had been of no help and they wanted no help. Of the entire group, 35% reported that they had received no help. Twenty-five percent reported they had received some help but not enough. Sixteen percent thought they had received about the right amount of guidance, and 23% could not say whether they had been helped or not.

In analyzing the reasons for these responses, it became evident that there was a lack of confidence in the clergyman's ability to comprehend the problems of business or to apply moral and ethical values to the complex world in which the businessman functions.

One religiously oriented personnel director of a large corporation stated: "I don't think the average clergyman knows enough about business to be specific." A young New York stock broker said: "The average clergyman has such a scant understanding of the U. S. economy that his intervention in this area would be a mistake."

One business executive put it in these words: "If ministers are to communicate, it would help if they knew something about the circumstances under which businessmen live and move, the pressures, the temptations to which they are subject, and the pitfalls and opportunities peculiar to their stations."

Lack of knowledge of what businessmen do and failure to realize what business is like, severely handicaps the minister's effort to reach and move an important segment of his congregation which, collectively, constitutes a key group in today's world."

Some of the questions which businessmen face, which they feel the clergy do not comprehend, are:

- As business grows larger and more complex, does its very size tend to erode or anesthetize our ethical standards?
- How can we preserve personal morality in the impersonal corporation?
- A business executive suffers from conflicting roles. Is the behavior expected of him as an economic man in conflict with the expectation of him as an ethical man?
- Has business become so complex and stratified that many of its ramifications are beyond the moral understanding of the businessman or the clergyman?
- Is there an increasing gray area where there are no clearly defined ethical rules or guidelines?

Some of the frustrations and failures which the clergy feel are equally well stated and clearly identified in recent literature. The classical example comes out of the recent anti-trust price-fixing scandal, involving the electrical industry. Raymond Gibson, formerly a pastor at Pittsfield, Massachusetts, where several of the General Electric executives live, commented on the confusion and bewilderment which the churches felt as they faced this staggering problem. Responsible corporate executives, trapped in the anti-trust suit, were members and officers of the churches of Pittsfield. The pastors and the churches sought to identify the role that religion should play in this tragic situation. Church families were involved, careers were at stake, trusted and loyal church officers were faced with prosecution.

Said pastor Gibson, "The sense of confusion was as marked in the churches and among the clergy as in the community at large. Throughout the whole turmoil, the irrelevance of the churches to the situation was evident. The pastors did not know what to say to the men in question—to either the "good guys" or the "bad guys." On the moral issue the churches were mute. No statement came from the Council of Churches which had been accustomed to take stands on issues of social concern. Both the "good guys" and the "bad guys" were members of churches, but to my knowledge no one of them came to his pastor to discuss the moral implication of what he had done or was doing.

"To each other, ministers confessed the sense of confusion they felt in regard to the moral issues, their inability to grasp the complexity of corporation decisions, their feeling that many of the issues involved were beyond reach of traditional standards of piety. They agreed that personal moral standards could do little to illuminate corporate actions and that no guidelines to corporate ethics exist which are readily acceptable—even to those concerned that action should be moral."

The silence of the churches created one or two impressions: that no moral issues were involved, or that moral issues were involved, but that guidance on those issues was not to be had. If the first impression is true, one must conclude the churches do not know enough; if the second is valid, it is apparent that they do not care enough. In either case, the impotence of the Pittsfield churches is a sign of the widening of the distance between "religion of the parish" and the pressing problems of today's work-a-day world.

While this is a classic example of the strange and distant worlds in which clergymen and business executives live, there are other similar but not so dramatic examples. In recent writings ministers complain that they have been forced into administrative responsibilities which are not the proper tasks of the ministry and for which they were never trained. They complain that they have become institutional managers, community chore boys, spiritual handy men, and that these obligations prevent them from being the professional spiritual counselors, wise observers of our times, critical judges of our generation.

Other ministers point out that the theological schools are turning out men whose general beliefs differ basically from those of their parishioners.

- The good news they preach is not the news the congregation wants to hear or is prepared to accept.
- One Episcopal minister confessed he had all but lost contact with his flock, except in the area of social events, charity affairs and pastoral counseling.

- A minister commented plaintively: "What I believe about God, man and the world, has no relevance to my congregation. They want a religion that will make them comfortable, that will reassure them that their way of life is right and will confirm their easy assumptions of superiority. The ministers of most denominations I talk to all have the same reactions."

As one reads the comments, confessions, and revelations of today's clergy, he feels the clergyman finds himself in an impossible position. While fighting to maintain a constructive ministry, he struggles like a drowning man who knows the current is too strong for him.

Many thoughtful laymen have a genuine concern about this breakdown in communication. A few suggestions have been made for bridging this gap. James Worthy, former vice-president of Sears, Roebuck & Company, suggests that many clergymen get their ideas of business and the businessman from the caricatures to be found in such books as *The Organization Man, Status Seekers, The Pyramid-Climbers*. Worthy believes that even though the curriculum of the theological seminary is already heavily burdened, there must be a new training for the clergyman, if he is going to comprehend the world of business and to be able to minister to the great body of business leaders and executives which make up an important part of our society. Worthy makes a strong appeal in these words: "When my minister says, 'Seek ye first the Kingdom of God,' I am sure he is talking not just about the time after working hours, nor is he asking the businessman to give up his economic role in favor of life in a cloister—but how does one first seek the Kingdom of God in the business world? I think it can be done, and I am sure it is inherently no more difficult in business than anywhere else, but it is the calling of the minister and the theologian to make religion relevant to all of life, and this is one phase of life they cannot afford to neglect. We must find ways to bring them and the businessmen together in creative dialogue."

Some executives have suggested that they would welcome regularly scheduled conferences or discussions between business executives and clergymen on the problems faced by leaders in the business world. They have indicated that they would like to sit down in a free atmosphere to share with thoughtful and knowledgeable clergymen some of the delicate problems, some of the complex questions for which there are no obvious answers. Thus, over a period of months, they believe the clergymen could become acquainted with the business world and corporate management. At the same time the business executive could become more familiar with the perspectives and insights of the clergy.

In some high level management conferences, it has been suggested that key clergymen be included in decision making processes of business. The automobile industry has suggested that clergy counselors for labor and management might be useful as a sort of conscience or ethical guide for the great decisions which involve the welfare and destiny of millions of people.

In some business circles it has been suggested that special training be set up for clergy in economics, social science, corporate management and executive decision making. Personnel directors are particularly sensitive to the criticism which the clergy offers, and would welcome the opportunity to familiarize the clergy with personnel policy, problems, principles, and procedures.

While most executives frown on the concept of a plant chaplain, businessmen in general welcome the assistance of the clergy who are well educated in business, economics and social science. Executives like the idea of the clergy meeting with businessmen in small discussion groups, where free discussion without pressure or acrimony can take place.

In all the problems that face our religious community, none seems greater at this moment than the gap which exists between the pulpit and the pew. ◻

Women in The Church: Comic Strip, Society Section or Front Page?

By Peggy Way

ARE the activities of women in the Church newsworthy? Or are they more closely akin to the comic strips and the society sections? Let us speak frankly.

Many view women's groups with a caricaturist's eye. There Helen Hokinson-like, big-bosomed and well meaning matriarchs invite men to their podium "to summarize the world situation, after which tea and cookies will be served."

Others relate women's groups to the society section. The First Church Rummage Sale is "covered" by at least an assistant editor of the Women's Sections of our metropolitan dailies. Pictures show long lines of people converging on the massive church structure to purchase discarded lamp shades and minks, tablecloths and earrings, the proceeds of which go to support a home missions program. In the remaining rural areas of our country, church sponsored bake sales, white elephants, and the making and selling of recipe calendars are reported under Social News.

This is manifestly unfair. Yet for those of us who believe that women's efforts in the contemporary world—*particularly within the Church*—belong on the front pages, there is far too much truth embedded in such stereotypes.

It is no secret within ministerial circles that numerous clergy do not know what to do with "their" women's group. Actually, the pastor may have very little to do with the structure, program or missionary outreach of these auxiliaries or guilds. From local circles through federated boards, they tend to chart their own course, set their own pace, establish their own patterns, and write their own theologies. The leadership is deeply entrenched and brooks no interference—particularly from pastors. A great deal of power is involved—financially and socially—and some pastors reluctantly find themselves treating the leadership in the women's organizations most cautiously, even if this means divesting themselves of their own prophetic role.

Such a situation breeds self-satisfaction, contentment with what exists, and great defensiveness at the slightest hint of criticism. Because of this it can be argued that women's groups impede church renewal as much, if not more, than any other ecclesiastical force, not only because of their structured power, but also because of their naivete regarding the real task of the Church in the contemporary world. Some members of the clergy have avowedly given up on women's groups and have made the decision to expend creative pastoral energies elsewhere until a new generation of women emerges.

There is much truth in this recognition of what might be called the "generational gap" in women's groups in the Church. Their primary appeal is to the older generation. Even its leaders complain of the lack of interest among younger age groups, and wonder where the necessary new leadership will come from. Put bluntly, the minister's wife may be the youngest woman in attendance, forced by virtue of her position to participate in a structure rooted in a genteel society where women did not work and were expected to "do good" through their church organizations.

But today's women do work, and even those who do not may prefer to spend their time with the PTA, the American Association of University Women, the League of Women Voters, a local drama group, or in part-time or even full-time educational pursuits. Moreover, a younger generation of women, accustomed to the give and take of conversation in a bisexual environment, are less apt to seek out the sexually segregated "proper" place for women which the Church provides. Yet even if they did choose—or felt they had to choose—church work, what would they find there?

They might well find: Lengthy discussions on the importance of saving trading stamps to get new kitchen equipment for the church. An assortment of "devotions," falteringly read from the many canned devotional booklets available through the various denominational presses, which are embarrassing if not irreverent to the person seeking a meaningful worship experience. Formal reports from "Love Note" and "Sunshine" Committees. (Please to bring one's old clothing to rummage sales, one's old toys to Christmas parties, one's old canned goods to donate to the poor.) I have attended Christmas meetings where the devotionals were almost scrapped because the group was having "so much fun" competing to see who could wrap the most beautiful gift. I have seen canned goods piled next to the altar as the sacrificial offering of the well dressed women who went from there to a delicious luncheon. They would also find: Speakers from the "mission field" who ride the denominational circuits on one-shot visits and encourage the old clothes-old toys-canned food syndrome. Overt expression of all possible prejudices and stereotypes concerning "the poor" and "the colored" during discussion of the problems of the new metropolis and after a devotional period emphasizing brotherhood.

Just as significant is what may not be found there. Certain groups of women are missing: single women in large numbers; working women, single and married; representatives of the younger college graduate groups; mothers whose children regularly attend the church Sunday School but whose budgets do not allow for the clothing or social accoutrements felt necessary for "circle" participation; and of course, Negroes or members of other minority or newcomer groups, frequently living closer to the church geographically than the older members, but assumed to want to be with "their own kind."

Other realities, more atmospheric in nature, may be missing: A sense of involvement in the social and political issues that lie behind the appeals to give old clothing, toys and food; a dynamic participation in the search to find out more about the changing world and the nature of meaningful existence within it; excitement (and the pain of responsibility) through searching after the reality of God in this world, and exultation (and humility) in worshipping this living God through a variety of contemporary and traditional worship experiences, whether carefully planned or spontaneously emerging.

Little things like these.

Our stereotypes of women's groups may contain too much truth. Perhaps that is why we do not like to look at them.

Yet even those who believe in such stereotypes must be helped to recognize them as only partial truths which mask other realities and potentialities. For example, it is often forgotten that most women in the Church are not only sincerely motivated, but *are doing precisely that which Church leadership over the past fifty years has encouraged and provided opportunities for them to do.*

It is a fact that formal Church leadership (need we state that it is predominantly male?) has counted on the women to raise money *in whatever ways they could;* to do "good works" *for the entire Church;* and to keep themselves occupied in their own organizations and *out of the sessions, vestries, church councils, presbyteries, etc. — where the real decisions concerning the Church are made.*

If women have honestly sought to do just this, then the words of the elderly woman who told me "I don't understand—I've given my life to the circles, and now the new pastor tells us that they are all wrong"—are indeed plaintive.

Traditional women's groups are often branded as irrelevant, irreverent and banal. *But they are no more so than the rest of the Church* and the truth is that the struggles for renewal now going on within them bespeak of the latent health of the *entire* Body of Christ.

Such struggles do exist. One takes its impetus from secular society where popular and serious literature has for some time now been re-evaluating the role of women in the contemporary world. The Church has been singularly silent. There are few groups which have selected *The Feminine Mystique* as study material, and few pastors or laymen that have contributed to the growing body of literature. But let us be clear that the issue is much deeper than just getting such discussion *inside* the churches. The real question is whether church women are helped *to go out into secular society,* strengthened by those understandings of feminine (and Christian) identity, sexuality, commitment and personhood which are a part of the Church's heritage—and whether they can carry the ministry of the Church beyond itself, into the world where it rightfully belongs.

Another struggle is going on wherever women are bold enough to question the purposes of their various home and foreign mission programs. Is hemming diapers around the lunch table really attacking the social realities of our time? Does the old clothes-toys-food syndrome reflect sacrificial giving or the seeking after cheap grace, far removed from the human and social realities of the receivers? Can a racially segregated Church and community—whether in suburbs or inner city— offer to Christian young people the type of life experiences most crucial to them? Does the Church's involvement in the city and in contemporary culture recognize that this is God's gift and challenge and not God's curse?

A third major area of struggle goes on at the organizational level where some women leaders are seeking to desegregate the traditional Church structures which relegate men to men's groups and women to women's groups. Contemporary emphasis upon the role of the laity does not discriminate between men and women, although of course they have different histories and unique roles to play. But in a society where women are as highly educated and professionally competent as their male counterparts, it is a vast waste of Church resources to keep them isolated except for token representation on governing bodies to present the "woman's point of view" for the men who really make the decisions.

These struggles are most encouraging and reflect the great potential which women have to offer to the total Church as it seeks after itself in God's emerging world. In fact, for every negative stereotype, or partial truth, put forth condemning women in the Church, I can offer a positive reality demonstrating the commitment, concern, contemporaneity and creativity of individual women in today's Church. They do not, however, always reflect the ongoing orientation and programs of *women's organizations,* which may remain lethargic, condescending or openly critical of women seeking after new ways in the service of the living Lord.

The focus of the discontented should not, then, be only upon one's personal repulsion with the canned devotions or the cheap graces of doing good works in isolation from the world. We should be more concerned with re-focusing the ministry of the Church upon the frightfully real questions that today's women —in and outside of the Church—*are* asking. How can I raise my children to be healthy and socially conscious persons, with a strong enough sense of identity to withstand and counter the negative aspects of contemporary pressures? What is the meaningful life for the widow—or the wife of the retired man, facing ten to twenty years of "leisure time?"

How does the single woman cope with her own sexuality in a world in the midst of a revolution in morals? How does one combine commitment to family with commitment to vocation— a tension brought about by the increased educational achievements of today's women? How can the housewife best stand with her husband, understanding his world and its fragmentation and helping him to keep whole even as she seeks for him to enter meaningfully into her more home-bound experiences? And how can a deeply personal religious faith be held in tension with profoundly significant social action in the name and with the strength of that Faith?

I offer a direct challenge to women's groups to address themselves to such questions, and assure them that the interest and capacity to encounter them is there.

Even the traditional organizational structures hold vast possibilities if they can be refocused. Put simply, the network of women's organizations is so tightly structured that the Church can readily get women together and communicate with them from the top on down. The question is whether these existing structures for communication have really been used to communicate about significant ideas and actions.

Why have there been no national "Wednesdays in Mississippi" programs sponsored by our nation's Church women? A secular group has sought to bring high ranking and socially acceptable women to Mississippi to meet with local women for discussion about the racial situation. With this existing structure being such an excellent vehicle for fund-raising, why have there been so few attempts on the part of Church women to demand and finance some of the many new social welfare programs being called for in the vast metropolitan areas of our country? What if the spirit of Jane Addams were so to penetrate these existing structures that persons within them reached out to become involved with real people—as she did—and to plan with them the new structures for mission that are clearly indicated?

The traditional concerns of women are another avenue of real potential. Many existing programs focus upon children and family life. What if these were helped to become less sentimental and moralistic and more related to the real problems of children and parents in the inner city—and in the world today? Suburban church women are as concerned about child rearing practices in contemporary society as are inner city mothers. What if church mothers—in interclass and interracial groupings—shared their mutual concerns, problems and answers, beginning with the children and inevitably moving into the related areas of civil rights, housing, education, politics and employment that could bring to life *as no other program* the nature of contemporary society and its demands on parents everywhere? We might note that this would not be asking women who pride themselves upon their maternal and home-maker's role to be *less* "feminine," *but to be more so,* raising questions about motherhood and the meaning of the home that express concern for children and families everywhere!

Another of the traditional concerns of women deals with physical facilities, their attractiveness and cleanliness. On two levels this could be redirected. *First,* they might focus more upon the nature of the Church and the meaning of ministry in their local churches, and less upon the need for new building programs and the various physical accoutrements that eat up so much of the average church budget. By so doing, they might discover, as many already have, that buildings have an accidental rather than intrinsic value in furthering the ministry of Christ in this world.

Second, if they are truly concerned about cleanliness, they might encourage inner city persons to work through local community organizations to demand better city services in sanitation, rodent extermination, alley cleanup, etc. They might ask those settlement houses which they seek to support if they are really working with local leadership in encouraging it to attack these problems, or if they are just perpetuating "nice" programs which are today being criticized even by professional social workers. And when they are embarrassed to find dirt in the buildings where home missions programs are located, they might ask if the program really belongs to the people and if they feel it is their responsibility or that of the suburban board and professional staff where they are not represented.

Women are a real power force in the Church. Once started, they cannot be "turned off." What if they "turned themselves on" to that which is generally recognized among contemporary church and social welfare leadership to be of the greatest significance, socially and theologically—and the two are not necessarily the same? Their activities would indeed become newsworthy, and their activities, whether or not marked as "Christian," would be covered on the front pages as well as the society sections. Even the caricaturists would be less condescending (as Helen Hokinson was) and the social and political caricaturists, the Bill Mauldins of our time, would need to recognize their historical importance.

Thus we see that, even as stereotypes may present uncomfortable truths, they may also mask the real caliber of women both *in* the Church and deeply wanting to be *of* the Church as it—through its laity—confronts the problems and opportunities of this world.

Several years ago, a woman philosopher writing in the Journal of Religion suggested that theology tends to reflect masculine rather than feminine experience. And why not? Theologians are overwhelmingly men!

She also suggested that major theological emphasis upon pride as the condition for human sin reflects the traditional nature of male existence as embodying aggressiveness and power. False pride and the temptation to misuse power thus create the masculine condition for sinfulness, and the theological plea is for greater humility and less confidence in one's own resources.

The situation is different for women. The nature of feminine existence has traditionally been more passive and self-denying. Yet the theological plea has emphasized even greater humility and self-abnegation. Few—if any—have recognized that *too little pride, rather than too much pride, may be the condition of feminine sinfulness.*

It is not a far step to suggest that the banality of much women's work in the Church is related to such a dynamic. In their false pride, men tend to protect women from the "real world" and in women's lack of pride, they tend to accept this and retreat into "safe" roles. But if women do this, they must then accept the stereotyping, condescending and sentimental view of their work held by many churchmen. And they are totally unprepared when a younger generation of Church leaders begins to look to them for programs of significance.

This dynamic affects all women in the Church. It is time to say openly that the Church treats its own professionally trained women, its Christian educators and pastors, as second class citizens. If this is so, it is no wonder that women's groups have followed the directions they have taken. The recently passed legislation assuring "equal pay for equal work" for women will be embarrassing to no organization more than the Church. But this is merely symbolic of the real gaps that exist between men and women Christians, whether in the various traditional ministries, or within the more recently emphasized ministry of the laity.

Here is where renewal must begin: *first*, in serious considerations of the meaning of the new responsibilities of the laity; and *second* in serious consideration of the role of women in the contemporary world and implications for this in professional and lay ministries within the Church.

We have for too long accepted definitions of femininity that emphasize physical attractiveness, submissiveness and intellectual vacuity, when actually the qualities of femininity quite transcend a particular role or appearance. A woman can be feminine whether she seeks after a career, combines a vocation with meaningful family life, or chooses to be a homemaker standing with her children and husband as a part of, and not apart from, their worlds.

Many of our conflicts concerning femininity are false conflicts. A women chooses not between a career and a family— but FOR being a person. And the man chooses not an aggressive career woman or a meek homemaker, but a full person who seeks after wholeness wherever she is. Such understandings, which have a profound theological base and significance, can help men and women more fully share together their common tasks as Christians in a world crying for their commitment, competencies, and the rich variety of their many gifts.

These discussions will provide more specific directions for renewal. First, women's groups will engage in self-evaluation, asking who is—and who is not—attending and why. They will ask what they are and are not doing and why. Such self-evaluation must lead into honest confrontation with pastors, denominational leaders, and leading women from outside the mainstream of women's work in the Church. It will be found that such topics as the nature of the Church and the nature of the ministry must be pursued; local seminary or denominational leaders can be of real help.

Second, through discussions women will find themselves asking their local churches to enter into similar penetrations into the role of the Church in contemporary society, and will ask the predominantly male governing bodies to isolate priorities and determine the best possible structures to minister to, in and with the world and its people. They may well lead local churches into deeper encounters with the contemporary situation and mission of the Church than has yet been accomplished.

Third, evaluation of home and foreign mission programs must receive particular attention. Pastors representing inner city ministries and experts from the social welfare field would be glad to meet with them to explore contemporary realities and trends and the ways in which particular programming must be transformed or created to be related to them. Women would have to grapple with the most crucial issues related to today's ministries: do they emphasize participation or philanthropy? mutuality or moral proclamation? profound graces of involvement or cheap graces of self-conscious good works? focus on issues and action or on navel-gazing study?

Fourth, it is crucial that such renewal not get bogged down in yet another study series. Someone has said that the Church has the best trained inactive army the world has ever seen. Certainly this is true of women's groups, which have for years been "studying" selected areas of home missions. At the same time individual women are afraid to go into the city alone.

But real learning can only come through involvement, which can then be meaningfully reflected upon. Representatives of women's groups can *at once* go into home mission programs as volunteers, bringing themselves and not just their old accoutrements. But they can also volunteer their time to civil rights organizations, to groups concerned about education in the inner city, to various public agencies dealing with child welfare, etc. They can then report back on what is really going on in the world, serving as Christian reporters *on* the world who are actually experiencing and thinking theologically *in* the world.

It is inevitable and not undesirable that women will continue to be caricatured. Done in the "right" places, it is indeed a sign that they have "made it." Society leaders shall continue to report on their efforts. They *should,* and how nice it would be if the pictures demonstrated the reality of interracial and interclass ventures, and if the write-ups focused on the issues being dealt with instead of the menus, the clothing worn, and the leader's names.

More important, the growing numbers of Christian laymen will demand front page coverage as citizens penetrating into the very fabric of secular society—not primarily to save it or redeem it, but to take it seriously, to act within it, and to reflect upon it as the only location for Christ's ministry in the contemporary world. ☐

PART TWO

DOES THE CHURCH NEED A NEW STRUCTURE?

The crisis facing today's Church goes beyond the issue of definition. Even if we could reach a consensus on definition, even if we agreed that the Church should be a servant people whose ministry is to the world, the question of the adequacy of present forms and structures would remain. Is the residential parish a suitable base from which to tackle the massive issues of the emerging metropolis? If laymen ought to form the vanguard of the Church's prophetic ministry, what structures and forms are needed to provide training and sustenance to a renewed laity? Is the Church as presently structured equipped to enter the world of work? Is Protestantism too institutionalized to permit significant changes? Should we work for renewal within the institution, or should we conclude with Gordon Cosby that the present forms of Protestantism have no future whatsoever? Finally, if we were to reject the present denominational pattern of Protestantism, how difficult would it be to alter the present habits and policies of denominations? These are some of the questions dealt with in this section. ☐

Structures For The New Era

By Don Benedict

THE continuing debate concerning the efficacy and relevance of the Church in its present structures is growing in intensity. We take turns blasting the Church and then the clergy for the growing ineffectiveness of the Church as an instrument of God's mission in the world. I do not believe that this criticism is bad but if it stops at the defense of one or the other, then little creativity will emerge from our present encounter. Rather we must see our present criticisms in the light of our historical situation. Years ago Reinhold Niebuhr said that we stand at the end of an era and on the brink of a new world powerless to be born. Historically we have moved on from the time when that statement was uttered. As long as we stood in the vacuum between the worlds we could calmly discuss the prospect of a new world. Now we are experiencing the birth pangs of a new epoch, and social, economic and political forces are ushering in a new era of history. The era born of the Protestant Reformation is coming to a screeching halt.

This new era of history, symbolized by the metropolis, is forcing both the Protestant and Catholic faiths to reflect anew on Biblical faith and the relation of the Gospel to the contemporary world. In a sense Protestantism itself was born out of a new reflection on the world as historically we moved from the Middle Ages into the emerging world of the Renaissance and the rise of the bourgeosie. We should not be shocked therefore if some radical changes are indicated when the present church confronts the emerging metropolis. Rather than spending our energy on either blame or defense of the church or the clergy let us focus on the *world,* which God has created and actively seeks to reconcile to Himself.

The primary focus of the Christian faith has always been and still is the arena of history. From the moment that God entered the world in human form through his Son, the imperative to deal with the stuff of history has been the central concern of the Christian faith. From the biblical account it is clear that Jesus was primarily concerned with such human matters as food, clothing, and justice. In fact it was God's concern for the *world* that resulted in the birth of Jesus. Moreover, concern for one's neighbor in the Biblical faith stands on a par with love of God.

Furthermore it is clear that Jesus, acting as the servant of God, did not call men to worship *Him* but rather called them into participation in history. "Come, *follow me*" was not a call to individual salvation by removal from historical reality but rather a call to participation and involvement. Jesus called men into the midst of the world to deal with men in the context of the social, political and economic forces of history. The church is thus a group of secular men and women called to be a Servant of God in history, which means within the structures of history. It is within these secular structures of life that *God's struggle* to make life human is found.

The shape of the historical struggle in which God seeks to make the world human will determine the type of structural instrument needed to respond to Christ's call. Twelve loosely knit disciples may be effective in one era and a huge hierachical, authoritative structure in another. The question for our day is: What structure will be the most faithful servant in this historical era of God's world? Is the shape and structure of the Church which emerged out of the Reformation era adequate in the new world which is now taking shape?

Many radical changes have occurred in the social, economic, and political structures of the world since the emergence of the Protestant Ethic. Democratic participation by the masses of people in public decisions was not in any sense basic to Luther's development of Christian ethics. He never dreamed of the degree to which public policy decisions now affect great masses of people. Consequently Protestantism has rarely taken seriously the responsibility for God's creation that is implied in representative government. Technology and urbanization have moved our society more and more toward corporate responsibility for vast areas of our social and economic life. The individual ethical act of the Good Samaritan has been replaced in our culture by an adequate city budget for ambulances. The responsibility for the education of our children now rests with a Board of Education which we elect or by a Board appointed by a Mayor whom we elect. Because the care of widows and orphans is a corporate responsibility of the state does not mean that it is any less our responsibility as the church. Yet, the

Protestant Church because of its undue concern for pietism and individual salvation has never seriously structured its life so as to act responsibly in these public sectors.

It is becoming increasingly clear that the corporate nature of public policy requires a new structure of the church which will seek in all humility to define the public interest in major issues affecting millions of God's children. Some of these major issues are now seen clearly in the modern metropolis. To enumerate a few: unemployment, integration, housing, public education, welfare, urban renewal and city planning. It is within the structures related to these areas of life that God's missionary activity takes place.

Another radical change in the structures of life which has occurred as a result of technology and urbanization is in the area of occupations. The modern work world for a vast number of people is a highly specialized job quite void of meaning and purpose. In the modern metropolis this work world is separated geographically from the residential world. Men tend to live in two worlds, a privatized world of their residence and a world of work. The Protestant Church, which is now tied by structure to the residential base, tends to reflect in its concern and program the privatized world of the home. *There is no doubt that this is an essential part of man's life in the world but it appears impossible from the geographical parish base for men to respond to the central issues of public policy or to penetrate the corporate structures of the world of work.* Many pastors in the residential church have developed expertness in dealing with the privitized sections of life but because of time and training find it impossible to break out of the parish based church into the broader corporate structures that play such a decisive role in our day.

Of course the geographical parish church is not the only structure which has emerged in response to Christ's call to servanthood in the world. In the Bible we know that Paul and Timothy probably purposely used the trade routes as a means of meeting mobile people. We also read of churches being organized among Caesar's household (probably slaves: first vocational groups) and some meeting in private homes as well as the catacombs. Many scholars believe that it was not until the 8th to the 10th century that the present concept of the parish church with a geographical area emerged. One can see that this structure was quite adequate at the time of the Reformation. In small German communities the church could be the center of both residential community and the world of work. Mass participation in government did not emerge until after Luther's death. In fact some scholars hold that while Luther developed the doctrine of the priesthood of all believers he was never forced to deal radically with the restructuring of the church but instead was able to have whole churches move from Catholicism to Protestantism with few changes in church structure.

If we are at a watershed of history and on the verge of a totally new society then it seems reasonable to believe that the major church structure developed ten centuries ago may well be called into question. Yet we must never be trapped into thinking that structures are primary. Form follows function. New structures will emerge in the life of the church only insofar as they are experiences of a new response to Christ's call to servanthood in the world. The role of the clergy, the role of the laity, a new piety and a new understanding of the word and the sacraments will emerge from encounter with the Metropolis. The church is a secular instrument and must be brought under the severe scrutiny of pragmatic evaluation. In its present shape and structure, is it equipped to carry on God's missionary activity in an urban technological culture?

The answer it seems to me is both *yes* and *no*. *Yes* in the sense that there is real validity to a residentially based congregation and *no* in the sense that a residentially based congregation finds it almost impossible to become relevant to either the work world of modern man or to questions of public policy.

In much of our recent condemnation of the existing residentially based congregations we have tended, I believe, to lose sight of the valid role of the local congregation. While we must be critical when people come to worship the institutional forms instead of God, we must see that the local residential area is also a part of God's world and hence an arena of God's missionary activity. Local residential groups too can be called into mission. This is especially true in city areas where many of the problems of Metropolis come to bear on the residential base such as inadequate public education, unsafe and unsanitary housing, blockbusting, integration, inadequate police protection and a host of others.

People can be called into mission residentially through local community organizations which seek to make the city human. The residential congregation also has a mission of personal servanthood to persons who are alienated from themselves and from their community. It has a teaching function especially with children and youth but also with adults in terms of their theological education. In most urban neighborhoods local congregations, if they have the necessary depth of acceptance, can assist youth and young adults to find identity and meaning in an apparently meaningless culture. Aged people too can be helped.

Many of the major battles of integration are going to be fought at the residential base and here the local congregation can, if it will, play a decisive role. Rather than write off the residential congregation we must see more clearly the nature of its missionary activity and help it to turn its attention toward the world. Better still there are probably some areas of the city where new congregations must be called into being on the basis of mission rather than remembrance. This is especially true in areas of new church development in the suburbs.

It is essential as new residential congregations are called into being that they must not be called on the basis of confessional belief. To call congregations together on this basis in our day is to deny the reality of our world. The basis of church membership must be more than acceptance of Christ as Lord and Savior. The basis of any call to membership must include a commitment to Servanthood in God's world.

At the same time we must recognize the limitations of residentially based congregations. While they can contribute to local citizen participation on local issues, there is still a need to develop cadres of knowledgeable laymen who are theologically alert and are committed to a particular public issue as their major missionary focus. Such a group might be called into being as a congregation around an issue like public education. Their task would be to become as knowledgeable as possible regarding public education and to search the scripture together for theological perspective on the question. They might purposely align themselves with many different groups in the city acting on this current issue. Out of this encounter may well develop a meaningful fellowship experience as they give themselves in thought and action to the problem.

Likewise groups of men and women might well address themselves to the world of work. We are probably going to spend many years exploring the ideological world of work before we see clearly the relevance of Christian ethics to the modern work situation. What is the ethic that informs the basic decisions of corporations and unions? In view of the growing interdependency of our whole economic situation, how is the public interest maintained among the giants of management, labor, and government? What are the complex ethical issues that businessmen, sometimes in spiritual agony, seek to solve? How can we call men to faithfulness in the context of their vocation? The Detroit Industrial Mission and now the Business and Industrial Project of the Chicago City Missionary Society is opening up this vast area of the world of work.

All of this is to say that as we enter a new era of civilization and the church faces God's new creation, the Metropolis, we must expect that residential congregations may emerge in new ways and that structures attempting to penetrate the world of public interest and the world of work will emerge. As this occurs I predict that great hostility and fear will develop. Pastors and church executives will be fearful that new structures will drain leadership and finances from local congregations. Pastors will be anxious about the apparent disloyalty of their men. Church extension executives of the denominations will be reluctant to begin new congregations along the pattern I have suggested. This will lead to the perpetuation of the current institutional cycle of buildings and programs which ignores the reality of the 20th Century technological urban revolution. Yet if the church is to move from Pietism, with its central focus on individual salvation and personal piety, to Servanthood, where the world is seen as the arena of God's activity in the midst of which the Church is called to serve, then some difficult and demanding decisions must be made by congregations and church mission boards. For years we have talked about the industrial revolution and the work of the laity in the world. Currently many denominations are exploring the nature of the urbanized world in which we live. It is my firm conviction that until we move from pamphlets and programs to an encounter with this world which we talk about we will never in our generation discover how ineffective our present structures of the church really are.

Rather than attacking and defending present church structures let the denominations take some of the most talented young rebels and explore today's world. The young men who are so critical of present institutions must produce some models of ministry that focus on God's missionary activity in the world. Similarly, pastors in residential congregations must seek to define and strengthen their ministry to the residential community and see to it that people at this level are likewise called into participation in God's activity rather than into a Cult of Remembrance. Perhaps most important of all is that the dialogue between residential and paraparochial situations must continue as we move into the new world where we shall face our God in stark reality. □

Into The World Of Work
By Bruce Hunt

IN practice the New England village seems to provide the model for the Church's relation to the economic order. Typically, the snow-white church building sat on the edge of the green, its bell tower dominating the surrounding commercial, governmental and educational enterprises. Thus the church stood aloof from the crass transactions of the market place yet rooted in the ordinary affairs of village life, symbolically in the world yet above it. During the flowering of New England culture, the clergyman was the best educated man in town and his counsel was sought on matters of public policy and communal morality.

Clearly this kind of village culture and this kind of clerical competence has long since disappeared in most of our communities. Still, such a change need not be the occasion for weeping after lost privileges, but for seeking an appropriate strategy. And a new strategy is imperative, if for no other reason, because the geographical and often spiritual gap between work and residence has placed an intolerable burden on the shoulders of the clergyman in the local parish. Some ministers, whose efforts are nothing short of heroic, attempt to stand with the men in their congregations by meeting groups of them in downtown restaurants, or by meeting them individually in plants and offices. The fact remains: The residential church is structurally unsuited to such occupational involvement, and there is already more than enough work to be done with families and neighborhood groups.

It will not do either to reduce the problem to a matter of language—"If only the minister spoke to me in my language rather than his own; if only he would use the jargon of the *Harvard Business Review* rather than the jargon of the theological textbooks." James Worthy is quite right in pointing out that preachments based solely on the language and insights of *The Organization Man* are superficial at best. Moreover, it is doubtful that an interdisciplinary seminary curriculum can go very far in bringing together the businessman and the clergyman, if the residential parish is taken as the normative structure of the Church.

The residential parish has become imperialistic, claiming the whole of a man's religious involvement, and seeking to bring all his life under the umbrella of its program. Now, I am not yet willing to join the chorus that wails over the corpse of the local church—it can do something; it cannot do everything. And it cannot consistently engage the man-at-work unless he happens to live and work in the same neighborhood and with the same people. Since such an arrangement is rather extraordinary these days, it ought not to provide the standard by which church life is determined.

Certain ground rules ought to undergird a new strategy:

• The primary goal must be the development and maintenance of an effective lay ministry in the world of work, and only incidentally the involvement of clergymen.

• Theologically, we must affirm that God is already active in the midst of the economic order, and not merely in the persons of those who confess Him, or "take Him there."

• The essential direction of ministry (that is, service, mutual support and corrective) will be from layman to layman, with the clergyman, if he is present at all, involved as a catalyst and not as an expert.

• Because geography seems to change the rules, meetings must take place in "secular" not "sacred" locations; that is, in plants and offices and not in the traditional church building.

• Local churches must find appropriate ways of supporting businessmen who minister in business and trade unionists who minister in the labor movement—probably at the expense of traditional programs.

Consequently, there will arise a kind of "dual loyalty," corresponding to the proper functional distinction between residence and employment. A man will remain a member of the "church that meets on the corner" but he will also be a member of the "church that meets in the office." I do not see this as a "disease of specialization." Sociologists have already noted that "the social life of urban man is continuously subdivided into areas of activity and interest, with each social segment lived out more or less independently of the rest," (Robert Dubin). If this be disease, then we are all infected.

How might these ground rules be applied? A brief analysis of one activity of the Chicago Business Industrial Project will illustrate. Nine young executives from a large Chicago corporation meet monthly from 4:00 to 8:00 in the company dining room. They represent a variety of staff and line positions in Sales, Finance, Production Control, Advertising, Personnel and Research. They have been gathered on an occupational rather than a confessional basis, and their expressed concern is to reflect on the "industrial problems of humanity"—to paraphrase a classic title by industrial relations expert, Elton Mayo.

The format for the meeting has evolved according to the interests of the group. At the start, in January, 1964, there was no structure, only the promise that the others would be there, that their discussion would be off the record, and that nothing was sacred. At present, the men themselves have determined to focus on "critical incidents" in the work place, that is brief written descriptions of decision making situations arising in the context of their occupational involvement. This procedure is certainly analogous to the case method of instruction used at a number of business schools. It means that discussion is specific—disturbingly so sometimes—rather than generalized; it also means that traditional beliefs are tested in the hard light of a concrete decision.

Using this approach, a variety of problems have been reviewed. These range from a concern for the treatment of a mentally disturbed subordinate to a heated argument over the justification for imposing the company's commitment to fair employment on its suppliers. In the normal course of events, questions of "the technological society" and the role of government in the economy have been vigorously debated. But surely these very "secular" problems are not outside the scope of divine will and action; indeed the group, consciously or unconsciously, is participating in the contemporary movement of God—this is, of course, a confession of faith that only some of them would acknowledge.

The job of the Chicago Business Industrial Project staff man, a theologically trained layman, is risky and ambiguous at best. He cannot pose as a religious expert or as the conscience of the group, especially in the light of the extraordinary sensitivity to ethical dilemmas which the group has thus far displayed. So he is an informal discussion leader, an "outsider" with perhaps a fresh point of view, who still knows a bit about what is going on "inside," and from time to time he may be called upon to interpret a particular situation in terms of an acknowledged theological perspective.

Most important, these meetings provide an occasion for reflection and review by business executives who are accustomed to spending most of their time "putting out brush fires." They also provide the structure by which a community—informal to be sure—of mutual support and criticism can grow. This, in fact, is happening and a model for ministry is being developed. ☐

Not Renewal, But Reformation
By Gordon Cosby

THE Christian Church will very soon exist as a minority people. The Church will be the diaspora—the Church in dispersion. As in earlier days, the way to the promised land may be through the wilderness.

We are going to have to give up the myth of Christendom because there is no longer any Christendom. It does not exist in the sense in which we have always thought of it. The population explosion is so great that the birth rate far exceeds the conversion rate.

We will have to give up the thinking and patterns we are accustomed to and try to get used to meeting the changing shapes of our culture.

Much more important than the patterns and the shape of the structures of a Church in dispersion is the spirit of the people. We still have to have the *charisma*—gift of the Spirit.

Throughout what follows, I will be using the term "structure" to mean the various phases of church life—the meetings, the committees, the organizational branches, all the organs and systems and plans of action through which the church exists and transmits her Life—in other words, the wineskins.

The present institutional structures of the Church must give place to new structures that will *be* the Church on mission. This conviction has come to me gradually—I have worked with it consciously for the past fifteen years and have been disturbed about it for the past three. Now I am convinced that the institutional structures that we know are not renewable. Even when there is renewal (and this goes on in many congregations) the stance of the Church almost always remains the same—a stance which is contrary to the very nature of a church committed to mission.

The Church, properly, does not engage in mission or merely send missionaries—the Church *is* mission and the congregation should express its life in the world. Its very structure must be changed to allow it to be itself. The Church, if it is to "go to all nations," must exist within the secular structures of mankind.

When the structures get as rigid and as resistant to change as they are now, perhaps the wisest strategy is not to try to renew them. It may be wiser stategy to bypass them and let God do with them what He will. The new structures which will appear may be so drastically different from the old as to constitute reform rather than renewal.

I would suggest that those of us who are called by the living God to belong to him will be on mission to his world and we will take the shape appropriate to our calling. These new shapes will throw light upon the path of those Christians who are still active in the old structures.

I want to clarify several things. The Holy Spirit is still at work in the old structures. People still get converted in them, and personal growth takes place in them. One reason it has been so difficult for me to come to the conclusion stated above is that I, myself, came to know Jesus Christ through the old structures. This reproach has been thrown at me time and again, and it is true. So it is with great reluctance that I have to say that I do not believe that the old structures can be renewed. This is not the way it seems to me God will work in our time.

Further, I am not writing *people* off when I make this statement. I am not expressing contempt; there are millions of people existing in the present structures and they are precious, loved children of God. They should be given the challenge of expressing their lives in mission.

I still intend to go, when invited, to the various seminaries in the country, and to the various churches, although I will have to be honest and say to them what I feel. It is in the seminaries and churches that we are most apt to discover the people who can develop the new shapes of the Church, for these are the people who have been working with these structures all their lives. Of all people, they are the ones who should know that the present structures do not work, that they are irrelevant.

I am not in any glib way writing off the whole Church. But I am saying that, as I now see it and as I now understand the nature of the world, the structures in which the Church is at present contained are irrelevant and simply do not allow the Church to be on mission. They hinder the proclamation of the Gospel rather than further it.

Now the question is, what will the Church look like when it is in the world on mission? What will be its shape? The only answer I can give is that I do not know. For several reasons I don't think anyone can know at this point. For one thing, the shape of the Church in our time or in any time is always determined by God.

The strategy, the tactics of the Church, the shape, the patterns, the structures in which it will express itself are all determined as a result of obedience to the living God. God leads his people day by day, moment by moment. He usually does not reveal his strategy a year, or five years ahead of time. Day by day He gives His people the wine, the life, the vitality of the gospel.

But this new wine always has to be put in new wineskins and this is always difficult, because people are always saying that the old wine is sound, good wine. We don't want to change. There is that which does not change—the givenness of the Gospel, the tradition we enter as a people of God, with Abraham, Isaac, Jacob, and all the constitutive events of the Christian faith.

But the wineskins, the shape, must be determined by God in this century and in every century. We will know varied patterns; God will work in numerous ways. We cannot absolutize any pattern. We can never say that we have the pattern for the twentieth century—hallelujah! God leads his people in every age in unpredictable ways.

Another possibility, very strange to me, and one which I had great difficulty coming to grips with, is that the shape of the church will be determined in large measure by the world. This idea was unthinkable to me at first. But the world of human beings determined the shape which God himself took when he came into the world that first Christmastime. The world determined the very form of the death of the Son of God.

Death by crucifixion was the world's way of getting rid of a disturber. Christ made himself vulnerable to the world. The Church is to be vulnerable to the world. It is to take the shape that the world needs. We are not to be protected by our own power structures which are so strong that the world cannot crucify us! Our faith says that the only way there can be rebirth is by death and that the Christian must always think in terms of death and resurrection.

The Church is in the world to die, not to develop power structures which protect it from any form of crucifixion.

The shape of the Church will be determined by the changing nature of the world itself. The Church must flow into the world, and its flow will take the shape of its channels. We must be willing to entertain wild hypotheses and fantastic possibilities. This is a very important frame of mind for people going into the wilderness.

Entertaining any possibility is quite different from recommending it; it is not saying, "This is what we must do." But several things occur to me.

- I think we ought to be open to the giving up of all professional ministries. It may be that I ought to earn my livelihood another way. Perhaps all of the ministers of a congregation should be engaged in a tent-making ministry and do their job in the life of the world.
- Another possibility is that of giving up all real estate. I think our present real estate serves us, but I think that a pilgrim people ought always to be open to the possibility of giving up all its real estate. If a bomb were to fall on this area we would have to be the Church without any real estate. The Church was the Church during the most vibrant period of its life, several hundred years, without real estate.
- Another possibility is that the Church might carry out its mission through small bands of people, just two or three or four or five, who would live out their lives in the midst of the world of business, the world of govermnent, the world of mass media, the medical world, the educational world—out there where they are making their tents, earning their living. Such little mission groups would be working at the problems of mass media, or on the issues relating to peace and prevention of war, or on race relations and housing, or with the poor, perhaps taking a vow of poverty.

I am not talking about little functional groups related to the local congregation. These mission groups of which I speak would *be* the local congregation. We need to redefine the meaning of congregation. "Where two or three are gathered together in my name, there am I in the midst of them."

What does it mean to gather—to "congregate"—in the name of Christ? It means to have been baptized into his nature. To have died with him and risen with him. It presupposes commitment. The congregation is a people to whom the Word of God is preached and to whom the sacraments are administered. These things do not have to be done by a professional minister; anyone who is appointed by that community of faith may do them.

The congregation of the future will live under a common discipline. It will take seriously not just the "gathering," but the going forth. Think of the freedom such a congregation would have—its mobility, with almost none of the paraphernalia or baggage of the institution—with all its energy available for its mission.

This is not to say that the past has nothing to contribute to the new shape. The experience of the past will be drawn upon more than it is at present. What I am describing is much more difficult than anything we have ever done. If anybody thinks this way is easier, he should find two or three people who really know what it means to be reconciled to one another and should inquire of them—people who are living out in their common life a prefiguration of what life ought to be in business, education, or medicine.

Such Christians will not say, "Come with me to church and maybe somebody there will be able to be the instrument of God's reconciliation." They will say instead, "You are now in church. We are right with you where you are. We will be the instrument of God's reconciliation to you here." They will say, "We are the Church. We are that miracle of God's grace." Of course this will not be said in just that way, but this is the conviction that will have to be expressed.

The tendency at present is almost always to try to relocate the people we would like to help. We say, "If I can just get them to church, everything will be all right."

What we must learn to say is: "Here we are. We are going to be with you right where you live. We're not going to pull you out of your environment; we're not going to make you a part of an institution to keep the institution going. And if we have to live with you in a tent for the rest of time and just witness to the fact that Jesus Christ, who is a servant, is at work in this world, we are going to make witness to that."

We begin to perceive the world not as a hostile place, but a place over which God is Lord. The world is different because

Christ came. It is not just the church that is different, the world is actually different. It is a reconciled world. And so the Christian is at home in it. He is at home, for example, in the world of government. The government is not a great hostile enemy, as we sometimes imagine. It is a place where people are, who have to be loved before they can be changed. And business is not just a place where dog eats dog; it is a good place where men live, a place of exciting opportunity for the Christian. Only as we really live in these structures of society, shall we be able to begin to demonstrate what life can be like in the world of government, of business.

The question then comes up, "How could we then belong to the *oikos,* the whole household of God?" Well, many of these little congregations would be able to send a representative to some other part of the world, or to bring a representative of the Church from India, the Congo, or Hong Kong, to live with us. Here is a group of doctors, or artists, or government people, who would bring a Christian from far away to be a part of their life together. Gathered thus, the whole *oikos* meets together. This would be possible, because practically all the financial giving would be available for mission.

Another way in which Christians would discover one another out yonder would emerge. We would encounter one another as people who have left their fortified positions and now only vaguely remember those strong and solid houses we once inhabited. We would really be a pilgrim people—a tent-dwelling people. We would recognize one another with an inward recognition.

Somebody says. "Aren't you afraid of what this would do? Everything would go to pieces. Thousands of new congregations. Hundreds of new denominations." Such a prospect doesn't worry me a bit, not one tiny bit. It is only a part of what I see as I try to discover the shape of the future. Maybe as you see what *you* see, and we get together under God, we will see something quite different from what either of us now sees. What is the shape to come? What is the shape of the Church for the world of tomorrow? ☐

The Denominational Dollar
By John R. Fry

LIKE the United States Government, the United Presbyterian Church in the U.S.A. has developed an apparently democratic way of making financial decisions. The United Presbyterians assign to their General Council the task of drawing up a budget suitable for proposing to the General Assembly. The General Assembly then hears the proposal and adopts the budget as its own. In that adopting vote the denomination as a whole is committed to the raising and expenditure of funds as outlined in the budget.

Now the General Council is a body of representatives—the senior executives of the program boards and agencies of the denomination, plus the Stated Clerk, plus the elected officers of the General Assembly, plus certain at-large ruling elders and clergymen elected by the General Assembly to serve specified terms. The General Council is an administrative body, sitting the year round, acting in behalf of the General Assembly which, as the executive body, sits but once a year. The General Council fulfills its budget-making task in the following way. A special committee is appointed to draft an initial budget proposal. Since the major boards and all of the agencies of the Church have an abiding interest in this crucial action, the committee is carefully representative. When it meets, the pie is cut, as the saying goes.

This affair is very gruelling because the boards and agencies must present their budget proposals *to one another,* not to the denomination at large or to particular churches. In such a gathering, glittering oratory and old fashioned stewardship appeals, as we can readily imagine, do not amount to much. Here professionals are dealing with professionals. Since each board presupposes, correctly, that the others will be going for all they can get, watchfulness prevails along with the tendency to overstress each individual request. Thus overstressed and pre-stuffed, the requests are quickly pared back to normal. In the end each board can say truthfully that it got pretty much what it expected to get.

But there are wheels within wheels, as Ezekiel said. For example, it is tacitly assumed that no board or agency will be required by its denominational fellows to cut back its operation.

Therefore no budget is ever new. No board or agency starts with a clean sheet of paper. Why is it that no board or agency can expect to be cut below its present level of expenditure? Let it be remembered that any coalition responsible for cutting one board's operation will live to face another year's committee and the possibility of other coalitions ready for revenge.

So it is always *existing levels* of operation that furnish the beginning of the budget. All else is embroidery. The main task of the committee is to determine how much embroidery the denomination will stand for (= pay for). At this point each board trots out its most glittering program ideas for inspection. More than likely, unofficial consensus has already been arrived at before the meeting between the major boards. They have already established understanding among themselves about which programs will receive the vote.

The committee's budget, the same as last year's, plus cautious embroidery, then comes before the General Council. Peeved boards and agencies have been known to petition the General Council for the inclusion of items cut by the committee, but this approach rarely succeeds. The General Council will discuss at length the budget *total,* and any new or very different items. But, traditionally, the General Council will approve the budget draft substantially as is. Again the understanding is that no cutbacks will be tolerable.

The reason for the no-cutback understanding is obvious. Most of the money allocated to boards and agencies pays for the salaries of staff, real estate, upkeep and program materials. A board must then fire staff, or reduce salaries; it must jeopardize real estate holdings; it must withdraw program materials, if there is to be any sort of cutback. Any one of these actions is painful. (One board of the denomination which does not receive all it believes it ought to receive has for years used its general (rainy day) funds rather than cut back its operation.)

Note: The boards of the denomination were created, historically, in order to superintend the denomination's mission enterprise and to produce "Sabbath School" materials. As the denomination saw other tasks that could only be done on a national (denomination-wide) basis, it created other boards and agencies, such as a Board of Pensions and a Council on Theological Education. Once created, these boards carried out their responsibilities as well as they could. But look at their position.

Their operations must be remandated every year. They must report to the General Assembly and are dependent on the General Assembly for their complete financial support. For this, and the reasons already suggested, the paramount question becomes one of what *image* to project to the General Assembly. Image components are responsibility, zeal and stability. This is a curious mixture, but it represents what the General Assembly as an aggregate group looks for and will support.

Inevitably a cut-back board or a stand-still board does not project a good image. Certain boards enjoy periodic ascendancy in General Assembly affections. The Commission on Ecumenical Mission and Relations has always enjoyed good favor. Between 1948 and 1956 the Board of Christian Education was the darling of the Assembly and since 1961 the Board of National Missions has come into a most favored position. The mechanics of winning and maintaining a favored position are of the sort that would require a C. N. Parkinson to describe adequately. The maneuvering for position, the proposing of daring new schemes, and the improvising of events at which vast achievement can be heralded are activities that each board engages in regularly. True, the boards were created to serve the grass roots needs of the Church—and they may—but their immediate and major preoccupation is with the business of staying alive and gaining priority position over each other.

The General Council may propose a budget to the General Assembly that is only slightly larger than the previous budget, or even with it, *but never less*. We must go ahead, you know, move forward. And these are precisely the terms used by the budget presenters at the General Assembly. Some new slogan is shaped, perhaps. And the embroidery on the budget—the new, exciting program—will be singled out for specific attention. At the 1964 Des Moines General Assembly, for instance, the appropriation of $500,000 for a Commission on Religion and Race was used to stir up enthusiasm for the entire $31,000,000 budget.

Now the General Assembly is composed of equal numbers of ruling elders (the laity) and clergymen, altogether about 825-850 persons. They are commissioned by other Presbyterians to sit as the highest judicatory of the denomination. This is quite an honor and a nice paid holiday on top of that, so there is vying back home over who gets to go. This means that new delegates always outnumber the veterans. The situation is ready made. Although the new people may feel equipped to declaim on nuclear disarmament or civil rights, they seldom have sufficient knowledge or courage to raise in public serious questions about the budget or any of its items. And, to be sure, the budget does not look questionable. The General Council, after all, is not composed of ninnies. It knows instinctively the highest amount it can propose without being challenged. The budget passes. The United Presbyterians, you see, have an orderly and democratic way of making financial decisions.

The problem of Church giving today is not located in the decision-making process as much as in the assumptions governing it. Let us take a layman's eye view of the matter. The United Presbyterian layman looking at the 1966 budget for his denomination sees that the "General Assembly General Missions Program" calls for $31,500,000. He also sees that in case the United Presbyterians give more than the budget calls for, there are plans in an "Advance Program" to spend another $1,500,000. He is no doubt comforted to know that denominational officials look ahead to any contingency.

On inspection he sees that by far the biggest category in the budget is $29.7 million: allocated for Christian Education ($4.4 million), Ecumenical Mission and Relation ($8.4 million), National Missions ($11.3 million), Pensions ($1.3 million), Theological Education ($2 million) and General Council ($2.1 million). Once he has begun thinking in millions he begins to drop the zeroes, you notice. Thus $4.4 million is comprehensible to him as $4.40. For Sunday School materials, $4.40 seems reasonable . . . $8.40 for overseas missions, $11.30 for National Missions and so on. All good work at a reasonable cost.

One assumption governing the decision-making process is that the layman, if given no information, will automatically approve the budget because he will tend psychologically to forget the zeroes and will have simply no idea of how much money one-million dollars *is*.

Another assumption is that the ordinary giver will take at labelled value the word "mission." This is a strong word. Some contemporary thinkers use the word as the equivalent of "ministry" and proceed to say that mission is what the whole Church does all of the time. Never mind about that. To the *giver,*

The Denominational Dollar :: 63

"mission" means Albert Schweitzer-types in Africa, in New York City, in Utah. "Mission" means underpaid and super-dedicated folks doing the Lord's work in behalf of all the under-dedicated in the local churches. Nothing is done, naturally, by the budget presenters to help the layman understand what the literal salary scale is or how few of the army of denominational workers are actually "in the field."

The presenters do not mention the number of bureaucrats engaged in administration only, who are paid in the general range of $15,000-$22,000 a year. The presenters never offer a breakdown showing the number of doctors, teachers, ministers, maintenance workers and other dedicated souls actually "helping others" in field locations as opposed to the number of administrators in Philadelphia and New York. The presenters do not mention that the cash outlay for administration and allied costs represents an estimated 70% of the total amount of money designated in the budget as a "general mission" item.

The assumption is that the layman will believe that the same rules that apply, by virtue of the pure food and drug laws, to commodities on the shelf apply also to the labels on church budgets. The assumption is that the word "mission" will evoke cash.

The third assumption regards the inability of the layman to give until suitably motivated. Bound up in this assumption is a very low doctrine of lay intelligence and a very high doctrine of lay vulnerability to pious expressions. It is never assumed that the General Assembly, through the General Council or the Stated Clerk, could communicate directly with every communicant member of the denomination and actually explain programs and aims and express what it hopes every member will contribute to the effort. It is never assumed that the individual communicant member has the combination of intellectual facility and personal financial responsibility necessary to make a response to the General Assembly program. It is always assumed that the layman must be enticed, thrilled, or otherwise made to feel the thundering drumbeats of history (each year) before he will give. One might suspect that the denominational officials in charge of raising money are secretly ashamed of their budget and would not trust it to go alone into the homes of United Presbyterians, unaccompanied by promotion and interpretation.

The denomination has moved beyond the simple provincialism of yesteryear in many areas. It has played a foremost role in ecumenical circles. It has played a strong part in supporting some phases of the civil rights struggle. The General Assembly has made a series of social pronouncements that are consistently on the side of sanity and Biblical religion. Moreover, some pretty tough-minded men have been employed on the major board staffs, men who know that provincial piety is a foe, not a friend of the denominations. Yet in spite of these remarkable evidences of maturity, the denomination retreats into the precincts of provincial piety when it has to raise money.

The denomination says that God wants the money. The denomination says that "you" are really getting somewhere as a Christian when "you" give MONEY (and time and talents). The denomination says that God's work in all parts of the world will flounder without full support. The Bible is used to make these denominational claims. So are flamboyant poems and saccharine stories. The denomination paints a picture that has a Schweitzer-type on one side. He features super-dedication. On the other side is "you"—the giver—who has under-dedication but also money. The Schweitzer-type and you-the-giver can be yoked together in common cause, and "your" money is the yoke.

The assumption under discussion here is that unless such a picture is painted, with Jesus vaguely in the background, the layman will not give.

All three assumptions are either presumptuous or pernicious and do not show a great denomination in its best light. The problem can be located very precisely in each instance. The problem concerns the absurd lengths to which denominational officials go in seeking to hide their administrative apparatus.

A patient reader can, of course, always go to the General Assembly Minutes. There he will find the names and numbers of all the players. There he will find his Schweitzer-types making $15,000 a year (and upwards). There he will find, if he is indeed patient, how much money is concretely devoted to administration and how much to program. By performing computations he can discover the amount of administrative money that is required to keep a program going. None of this financial material is secret. But the denomination officials are loath to broadcast this financial information beyond the pages of the General Assembly Minutes, which is hardly a best seller.

It might prove very thrilling to document the real financial facts of a mighty denomination, but it would actually accomplish nothing since the denomination exposes its financial facts each year. I do not believe that the administrative apparatus used by denominational officials to do this business is bad or wasteful. But I do have the distinct impression that *they* do not want laymen to know what is going on because they feel the layman will find administrative apparatus bad and wasteful. I have an undocumentable suspicion that denomination officials are secretly uneasy about the whole operation, as I previously have noted.

This is precisely the problem: the denomination seems to want to delude itself. Its officials and its membership apparently want to believe that all they have is a simple little $31.5 million mission enterprise. They share the fantasy that they are not an ecclesiastical business juggernaut.

How can it be that a board secretary, carrying all the major credit cards, traveling all over the world for the church, administering a section of the board's budget that is, let us say, $10 million, earning a salary of $20,000 a year, attending conferences, making decisions endlessly—how can it be that this fellow wants to and does actually delude himself into believing that he is not operating an ecclesiastical business? The availability of phychiatric categories is very tempting at this point, but ultimately a psychiatric answer to this puzzle would be less than fully fruitful. Since the answer is ecclesiastical, let us switch to ecclesiastical categories.

It is possible for him to delude himself by performing the following operations: He personifies the budget he administers. He is not spending money. He is working with people. He sees the whole denomination as mission, therefore he must be on mission. Moreover, the servants of the Lord in the field, whose salaries fall under his administrative care, could not function without him. This tricky way of perceiving is familiar. These tricky perceptions are similar to the assumptions made, in the budget-securing process, about the layman-giver. They are an attempt to ring from the reality of the huge operation a few drops of pure significance. They represent an attempt to wrestle an entire denomination across the faithful dividing line mentioned in Matthew 25 from the goat to the sheep-side of the Heavenly Kingdom. They represent, then, a refusal to believe that a complex bureaucratically organized denomination is credible as a $31,500,000 enterprise.

Perhaps other denominations suffer from self-delusion, too. I do not know. I do know that United Presbyterian officials do. They act like polished, politically sharp, institutionally aggressive folks who know the facts of life. They are very realistic about themselves. Each board puts itself and its future first. Each board protects itself from the other boards. *The safety of the institutions within the institution is a paramount concern.* To begin a budget meeting by questioning whether there should *be* a board of National Missions or a Board of Christian Education is sheerly unthinkable. The officials are, in a word, tough. They are real professionals. They know their business. But they act one way and talk another. They talk as if everything they do is: feeding the hungry, clothing the naked, healing the sick, visiting the imprisoned and preaching the Gospel. This is manifestly absurd. The actuality is real.

The point of this article now can be elaborated. The denomination could, within its orderly and democratic financial decision-making process, *reconstruct itself* so that it would actually be a $31,500,000, or $61,800,000 a year mission enterprise.

The denomination could reconstruct its national staff so that a few people would be given more administrative power and a great many presently employed people fired.

The denomination could maintain an allegiance to the poor by actually giving them money, and could open dozens of hospitals a year with the savings on airline travel that would be gained by firing the staff.

The denomination could even (one trembles in considering the possibility) forget the archaic categories in which it normatively pictures "mission" and begin working out a sophisticated strategy of special ministries that have something to do with the contemporary world. Then, instead of burying the amounts of money now given toward the creation of community organizations, for instance, it might devise the creations of dozens of community organizations as the crucial and most expensive single item in the whole budget.

The denomination could, to use a very *out* expression, become relevant. Or, failing that, the denomination could do everything that it deludes itself into believing (at budget-searching time) that it is presently doing, (i.e. mission in archaic terms), but only if it makes one critical decision, namely, that it cannot afford the luxury of its national staff.

But I do not believe the denomination will make such a decision. Therefore, with its positive, regularly affirmed commitment to the existing bureaucratic structures as a starting point for looking into the future, it will content itself with doing poorly what it says it wants to do well. □

PART THREE

DOES THE LOCAL CHURCH HAVE A FUTURE?

One would almost conclude from the previous sections—particularly from Gordon Cosby's manifesto—that the local congregation is not merely dying, but that it is dead. This section offers three case studies of widely differing local congregations that have experienced a measure of new life. But the conditions of new life are quite definite. In every case vigorous and sustained pastoral leadership emerges as a determinative factor. The willingness of laymen to reject the temptations of popular religiosity is also evident. In two out of three congregations examined, there has been a decision to concentrate on specific tasks at the expense of other possible activities. Thus the conclusion of this section may well be that the local congregation is indeed a limited instrument of mission, however necessary. There are things it can do and things it cannot do. The ultimate question involves the extent to which the positive elements in these case studies can be transplanted to other local settings. □

Sainthood Before Strategy

By Jared J. Rardin

GORDON Cosby, minister of the Church of the Saviour, Washington, D. C., has said that "the Church as we know it in our time must go. . . . I am now on the side of feeling that the institutional structures are not renewable." Some have been attracted to the pole represented by Mr. Cosby; most of us have—out of cowardice or conviction—placed our hope with the would-be renewers of the institutional forms.

As a person who first had the privilege of a year's participation in the Church of the Saviour, and since then has been associated with Bob Raines and Ted Loder at The First Methodist Church of Germantown (Pa.), I have sometimes felt the tension keenly. That little ecumenical church back in D. C.—whose minister is convinced of the unrenewability of the structures—is itself probably the clearest witness in our time to what a renewed church might look like. Yet I now serve, with increasing encouragement and hope, in this thoroughly "institutional" Methodist structure—a church, interestingly enough, which Gordon Cosby acknowledged to me to be as likely as any to "prove him wrong."

No perceptive visitor to First Methodist Church would conclude that Mr. Cosby was going to be proved wrong by next week. There are many marks of disobedience, and shortcomings at all levels of theology and practice. Yet this church does offer a great many hopeful signs, and since I've not been around long enough to be responsible for the good things going on, I feel free to observe them with hearty enthusiasm.

First, though, a paragraph or two for definition and focus are in order. The very word 'renewal' has the seeds of arrogance whenever it is allowed to suggest our human making-new of what has already been given by God. By 'renewal' I would want to suggest that process (which is always going on) by which the Church is enabled to discover the forms of Christian nurture and mission which are as faithful to the Gospel as they are appropriate to the times. With regard to this Gospel, renewal essentially means recovery; with regard to the structures, reformation; and with regard to the world, relevance. To the extent that renewal involves these elements, it has its vital

Sainthood Before Strategy

and authentic origins in repentance, that 'godly grief' over our aimlessness and sin, that turning back to the sovereign God who makes all things new.

Most of us would be quick to acknowledge that renewal is as much a gift as the original Gift which inspires it, but we turn right back to the moving about of our structural furniture or vigorous efforts to "create *koinonia*." Indeed, in our haste to replace the old structures we often end up making golden calves of our new (or wish-dreamed) ones. Renewal therefore seems to me to be more properly a matter of sainthood than of strategy. "The increase among men of the love of God and neighbor" remains a better criterion of church effectiveness and renewal than our questions about structure.

Further, the sociologists have made us aware, if Church history hadn't already, that institutions, like the poor, we shall always have with us. Indeed, it seems we shall always have poor institutions with us, since it is quite clear that "Institutions can never conserve without betraying the movements from which they proceed." So in all our talk of 'structures' and 'institutions' we shall need to be more concerned for their *flexibility* and *integrity* than for their replacement or abandonment. With the Bishop of Woolwich we acknowledge that the reformers and the reactionaries, the renewers and the conservers each exist by the grace of the other.

Even with these qualifications the question remains: "Can the old wineskins hold new wine?" I am tempted to answer, "Of course they can . . . if you have a thousand loyal and creative members, a budget in the hundred-thousand-dollar range, four reasonably effective ministers, and—perhaps most essential—a changing neighborhood!" These factors represent some of the resources for renewal within this particular local congregation, and the evidence of their impact is impressive enough to be noted in some detail:

1. *The preparation of persons for meaningful membership* has been re-emphasized and significantly upgraded by the participation of laymen and co-trainers. (The ministers give brief lectures at each of the six meetings, then are politely but firmly dismissed while the laymen lead a corrective discussion.)

2. Several *"Koinonia groups,"* small home-based fellowships living under disciplines of Bible study and personal growth,

have been formed (some as a direct response to the new-member training groups). Two of the church's official commissions are now using some of the small-group structures, and two others are "listening to the world" by focusing their study on God's Word as it comes to the church through the world of novel and drama.

Reasonably frequent retreats have helped extend this context of nurture, and out of one such retreat was raised up a covenant group to combine *koinonia* and *diakonia* (mission). It is especially noteworthy that one of the ministers was alert and flexible enough to offer a new structure appropriate to the needs and commitment of these people.

This group, sharing a fairly stiff covenant of study, involvement, and Christian growth, has purchased and renovated a house in a depressed section of lower Germantown. Operating on the periphery of the church, but increasingly with its knowledge and interest, the "Covenant House" folks are seeking to be equipped for "a ministry of being there," and of making available to the neighborhood the gifts of the members living in the house and of those who sustain them.

3. *An ongoing lectionary* is provided for the congregation, partly to encourage regular congregational exposure to the Word, and partly to defend the Word against the preacher's whims. We have no idea how widely (or narrowly) it is being used, but feel it helps to communicate the sense that Bible study is elemental rather than optional for the Christian.

4. *The increase in mission* and responsible involvement in the community has been significant. The establishment of a tutoring program, a teen-age coffee-house, some racial integration, and extensive work with community leaders, all point to the growth of *diakonia* in our midst. New members are asked to specify a regular community involvement (PTA, neighborhood council, political group, etc.) along with their commitment to a task within the church. And mission-mindedness was most recently reflected in a decision to double the traditional Thanksgiving offering (for a Puerto Rico missionary) in order to free the Easter offering for local mission.

5. *The doors of the church are opening wider.* The chapel facing busy Germantown Avenue is now open 24 hours a day. Tutoring and basketball groups are in and out of the building every afternoon and evening. Most recently, an old Sunday

SAINTHOOD BEFORE STRATEGY : : 73

School room in the rear of the educational wing was converted to house "The Glass Door," a teen-age snack shop operated by a committed and disciplined core of church members and youth. One of the remarkable things about this venture—this 'new structure'—is its emergence directly from the 'old structures.' Virtually every commission in the church has had an interested voice in encouraging and a generous hand in sustaining the program, yet without restricting its freedom.

6. *Stiff breezes of ecumenicity* refresh the atmosphere here. The word "Christian" is substituted for "Methodist" in church membership vows. First Church leadership—lay and clerical—is significant in local ecumenical doings. Most impressive is the fact that several members are involved with other Protestants and Roman Catholics in the establishment of "Wellsprings," an ecumenical retreat center for the Philadelphia metropolitan area.

7. Finally, it seems fair to say that there exists an encouraging proportion of church attendance, a high degree of general vitality and excitement, a steady stream of incoming younger adults (some from nearby churches), consistently fine preaching by the co-ministers, and most important: significantly changed lives.

These marks of renewal must be seen in the context of a congregation that has *always* been remarkable. A high level of flexibility and openness is deep in the tradition of First Church. (The acceptance—financial consequences and all—of the co-ministry plan is a good indication of this resilience.) A strong tradition of independence within the denominational machinery has increased the opportunity to experiment. A deep loyalty of members to the church has seen it through more than one crisis precipitated by the 'radical thrusts' and inevitable mistakes of its ministers. Perhaps most important, a marvelous vitality and richness of worship has been inherited rather than achieved by the present ministry.

I describe all these things, not to praise a church or to prove a point, but to convey as strongly and specifically as I can a sense of real possibility about 'renewal' within old and sometimes creaky structures. Doubtless many congregations could claim the same sorts of evidence, probably achieved in the face of much greater odds.

Another value of describing progress is to highlight what is still wanting. Despite the evidence displayed above, there remain some observations in the spirit of Jesus' rejoinder to the rich young man: "One thing thou lackest."

For one thing, the ministry of the laity has not been vigorously or systematically encouraged. The size and status of the church bring a pressure for "quality" which makes the ministers reluctant to turn over more of their responsibilities, and the laymen reluctant to assume them. The very co-ministry arrangement, for all its vitality and value in preaching and pastoral leadership, may be something of a deterrent to the development of more significant lay ministry.

This observation should not be confused with any implication that we haven't some wonderfully "salty Christians" and significant lay penetration into the structures of the city—we have many and much! I am only suggesting that, like most ministers, we find it a little harder to enable lay leadership than just to run things ourselves. We still seem to lack some of the capacity—as ministers and laymen—to demonstrate to each member that he has gifts vital to the whole Body, and to help him get better equipped for his special ministries.

We are still wishy-washy about our doctrine of the Church and the meaning of membership. I continue to marvel at the radical integrity which the Church of the Saviour invites—and gets—in its members. If the rest of us are going to shrink from offering such preparation and expecting such commitment, then we are faced with the greater task of offering and making desirable some non-required structures of growth and discipleship.

Dr. Claude Welch (whose affiliation with our church is another of its resources) keeps reminding us that the Church is defined by its Center and not by its circumference. The image is greatly helpful, but my impression has been that membership discipline at the circumference may be the best assurance of more total focus on the Center. It remains to be seen, by me at least, whether such a focus can be accomplished by context rather than covenant.

These categories are still at the structure-and-strategy level. To some degree they can be dealt with by determination and experimentation. The more telling deficiencies are as hard to describe as their remedies are to prescribe, but I perceive them as follows:

1. *We are not free from "hubris" and "henotheism,"* from pride and idolatry. (The present essay will suffice as Exhibit A.) The degree of our renewal is still being measured, by others as well as ourselves, in relation to other congregations, most of which haven't comparable resources in either heritage or budget; we wait to learn that the criteria for such assessments are God's, by whose standards we must look sadly unrepentant and unrenewed. Our renewal seems to lack the dimension of repentance. We may move on to a more significant level when we accept responsibility for the deterioration of the neighborhood before trying to participate in its renewal, when we acknowledge our continuing incapacity to love each other before we attempt to live as reconcilers in the world.

Henotheism, the inevitable corollary of hubris, is H. Richard Niebuhr's devastating term for "the worship of one god who is however the god of an ingroup rather than the ground of all being." First Church awaits a deeper conversion from its henotheism, for the present limited range of class, race, and condition in our congregation bespeaks a lingering commitment to a middle-class god. We are guilty enough of pointing to ourselves and our accomplishments rather than to the sovereign God, but even when we do point beyond ourselves it is most often toward a god who is too small. So we suffer in turn some of the smallness and defensiveness which comes of shrinking God down to our size.

2. We also have not really learned how to provide a pervasive, compelling, enabling context for "continuing growth in grace." Whatever is meant by "deepening the response to God's grace" and "embodying the Gospel," we don't know very much about the ways to give shape and urgency to them. They remain an optional luxury for those who wish to indulge, rather than a persuasive expectation that God waits to work in us far more than we could ask or imagine. The ministry of ours or any church needs charismatic persons, yet we lament the shortage of them rather than provide for their discovery and development. We might well begin our renewal of repentance by confessing our failure to call forth in the persons given to our care their fullest gifts of grace.

The very preparation of this essay has deepened my encouragement that whatever we mean by renewal can be and is already taking place inside our old structures. I emerge with more conviction that the question about "renewability" is a distraction from the main issues; I grow tired of the oft-heard lament, "Sure, Cosby can do it because he started over from scratch," or a cry I am beginning to hear, "First Methodist, Germantown, can do it because of all its resources and tradition of freedom."

Perhaps we are all best served by Bill Webber's knowing advice to a smart-alecky seminarian (me): "You don't have to worry about whether the wineskins are old or new; just be as sure as you can that you're pouring new wine into them. Then if they break you can start to worry about getting new ones."

I grow increasingly convinced that there is nothing in this Germantown situation which is significantly blocking renewal *except myself* and the individual Christians who, like me, are not ready to be renewed by repentance and to trust God's power to make worldly saints of us. If the structural issue, as I have tried to argue, is flexibility, the personal issue is our discovery that life is gracious at its heart.

Renewal calls more loudly now for saints than for scribes or strategists, though I am reminded that sainthood may well include gifts of communication and tactics. The reshaping will follow on repentance, the growth will follow the grace, and the sovereignty of God will shape and judge our structures. □

Study And Faith in Suburbia

By Stephen C. Rose

"WELL, I suppose you'd have to say it means the Golden Rule," the businessman responded when asked the meaning of Christianity. The same question was asked of a minister. "It would take hours to explain it," he replied. "It's summed up in John's 'God so loved the world that He gave His only begotten Son . . .,' but I'd have to go into the Old Testament to explain the need for a Messiah and spend some time on Original Sin and then deal with the Church as the Body of Christ, and then of course, the Trinity would have to be understood in terms of . . ."

And thus the chasm between layman and minister deepens. Through little fault of his own, the layman knows next to nothing about his faith, the Bible, or theology. The minister sits in his library and ponders the problem of "speaking so the layman will understand." Like the nuclear physicist at the tea-party, the minister is sometimes at a loss for words, at least when it comes to expounding the deeper meanings of Christian faith. Some churches have recognized that lay education is a top priority, but the vast majority remain Biblically and theologically illiterate. Laymen admit this; so do clergymen. But the chasm still exists. The sensitive businessman will tell you that the Golden Rule is not a sufficient guide in the midst of the intense problems of economic life. And, while the minister may nod politely when the layman tells him that Christianity equals the Golden Rule, he would never make the same statement among his theological colleagues.

In a suburb of Little Rock, Arkansas, there is a church whose minister openly denounces the illiteracy of laymen, and whose laymen demand that they be taught at the same level as seminary students. The Westover Hills Presbyterian Church would be a pleasant exception which proves the rule were it not for two sobering facts: the minister of this church seems no different— in terms of education, personality, leadership ability—than countless other ministers; the congregation is no different than countless other suburban congregations. The church is exceptional, but Westover Hills has merely tapped the potential that exists in any middle-to-upper-middle class suburban church membership. It is for these reasons that Westover Hills represents an important chapter in the story of renewal in suburbia.

Fifteen years ago, the Reverend Richard B. Hardie, Jr. moved to Little Rock with a degree from Union Theological Seminary (Richmond, Va.) and a call to start a church in a fast growing suburb.

The laymen of Westover Hills elected to keep building at a minimum. The original sanctuary remains. Money that might have gone into more sumptuous facilities is given away or plowed into the educational budget. The goal is to give one dollar away for every dollar spent on the church and its program.

Some churches have put excessive amounts of energy into questionable building campaigns. A mid-western church is building a chapel to add to its already large plant at a cost of $100,000, an activity which one layman privately calls "keeping up with the Joneses," the Joneses being the church next door which recently erected a modern administration building.) Some congregations emphasize church fairs, bazaars, bake sales, and other time-consuming money-raising activities. The financial policy of Westover Hills is explicitly stated on the church bulletin:

> The program of this Church is supported entirely by the contributions of its communicants to one unified operating budget, with each communicant being asked for one pledge annually to that budget. We take no special offerings of any kind; no money is solicited from the public; no funds are sought through sponsoring entertainments, sales of goods, dinners or other devices.

Dr. Hardie explains that this policy has freed laymen to study the faith, an activity which has top priority at Westover Hills.

The church has 750 members and a Sunday School enrollment of 450. Such figures are typical of many suburban churches. Here are some less typical statistics: One-hundred laymen teach in the Sunday school; an additional 175 members are involved in weekly study of one of seven subjects; the church's twelve women's groups meet only once a month, and then it is for two and one-half hours of Bible study.

What many laymen may feel privately, Westover Hills laymen admit in a mimeographed prospectus of the seven adult courses the church offers (all taught by teams of laymen): "During the last few generations we Protestants have tended to cut and trim Christianity to fit the optimistic, progressive temper of our modern cultural tradition. One fundamental feature of this tradition is the belief that there is nothing wrong with human beings that additional knowledge, wider education, and better scientific techniques cannot cope with. . . . The Bible does not agree with us."

And so the arduous process begins. Instead of topical, hit-or-miss sermons, Hardie "preaches through" the books of the Bible, taking a small text each Sunday and forcing the congregation to, as he puts it, "argue with the Bible, not me." Laymen are asked to read the weekly passages and, twice each year, an intensive week of Biblical and theological study is programmed with outside assistance from prominent seminary professors. In order to keep their pastor in preaching trim, Westover Hills frees him each summer to return to school for further study.

Hardie's preaching does not lend itself to editing. It is a conscious unity and the church is filled each Sunday for two services by laymen who wish to find their way through Philippians, Romans, and Revelation. Some samples from Hardie's series of Phillippians sermons:

- Paul is "blasting the pretensions of our day that so piously try to build a wall against the Christian conscience . . . But after I have said this, it is not my role as your minister to tell you what is vital. It is my role to open up this book and let you see what it calls you to . . ."

- "When Paul says 'with full courage' it is the Greek word for 'boldness or speech': I will not back down one iota . . . for my own personal safety."

- "The word Paul uses for 'citizens' of the Kingdom of Heaven is the same root word that we get 'politics' from. When the cry goes up in the Church, 'No politics!' it is usually the 'cry of the devil'."

- "I see in myself, and in you, a tendency to presume upon the goodness of God. How often do we look down our liberated noses at our legalistic brethren, never thinking of how we turn our Christian liberty into license."

This emphasis on the Bible results not in escape, but involvement. During the Little Rock school crisis, Westover Hills laymen bought (and signed) a full-page newspaper ad calling for tolerance and reason in the integrating of Central High School. When schools were closed, the same laymen pounded the pavements in the successful attempt to open them again.

The program of the church is based on a single premise: a church exists to proclaim the faith. This means intensive study, a willingness to open oneself to God's Spirit, and the desire to render service in both public and private life. Suburban churches have been criticized for their tremendous activity. Westover Hills has scaled down activities, partly because fund-raising no longer depends on time-consuming projects.

According to Hardie, "We are trying to see whether we can bring new life into a typical church structure. We're experimenting at how to use the structure intelligently." On the subject of lay intellect, he adds: "We're underselling the ability of suburban church members to deal with Biblical and theological content."

Hardie continues, "We ministers have spent too much time teaching people right and wrong. We should be teaching them how to make a decision through faith. We're trying to get people to stumble over the right stumbling block—that God became man and dwelt among us. Most people have had no chance to say yes or no to this. They've felt their problems were bigger than those the Church was dealing with."

What are some of the barriers to effective ministry? One of the greatest, according to Hardie, is the difficulty of convincing people of the Biblical fact that "we exist for one another and for the world." The American idea is that we should all stand on our own two feet. "It's hard to get people to accept help."

One of the factors which has helped Westover Hills' growth has been Hardie's long-term ministry. The length of one's ministry in a single church is always a debating point. How soon does a clergyman become "stale"? Hardie feels it is impossible to do an adequate job of education in less than five years. On the other hand, he feels he could leave now, although he has no intention of leaving, because laymen have become such active participants in the educational program.

The seven courses currently taken by Westover Hills members give some indication of the depth of lay involvement. The course in theology for laymen is dedicated to eliminating "flabby tolerance and vague thinking about God and the life of faith." The course on Christian faith begins by examining "some of the idolatries of our modern culture which make an impact on the outlook and attitudes of Christians." Another course deals with the Protestant and politics, yet another with the Apostle Paul. The Bible course emphasizes that belief in Biblical authority does not mean "accepting the Bible as a repository of "prooftexts'."

Hardie does not claim success. He seems too involved in next Sunday's sermon, or the coming week of theological study, or the possibility that another layman in the congregation will suddenly see the potential for deep meaning inherent in Christian faith. □

Toward A Religionless Church For A Secular World

By Howard Moody

TODAY'S Church may be standing at a fateful crossroads in her history—unable to resurrect traditions of the past and likewise unable to sense the Judgment implied by her present irrelevance to the world. We are the captives of institutional images and ecclesiastical structures. When one serves on many of the committees of the religious establishment (those ingenious formats by which the Church pretends to be critical and creative) one soon learns that the defensive posture of the institution gives the lie to all our talk about radical reformation. Despite the flood of jargon about renewal in the last decade, precious little has happened to the Church as we have known it.

Isn't it somewhat pitiful to note, after years of untold books, conferences, and creative thought about *renewal,* that the only concrete examples are a few once-hopeful experiments: East Harlem Protestant Parish, the Church of the Savior, and a few scattered "experimental ministries"? Albert van den Heuvel's assessment of this sad situation is pertinent: "When we look back at the period since 1945 we see the renewal movement imprisoned in carefully defined and eternal experiments which were never allowed to become a strategy. We see courageous new initiatives domesticated and others stopped because they were dangerous; some institutionalized and only a handful being still lonely and full of despair, swimming against the stream . . ."

This impasse is international in scope. For the past few years working committees on The Missionary Structure of the Congregation, appointed by the World Council of Churches, have turned their guns on the Church, and the "establishment" is still reeling and smarting under the attack. This raises the question whether an effective renewal movement can even function within the present structures of the Church.

Hardly noticed in the midst of this all-smoke-but-no-fire renewal furor is the fact that we are passing through a theological revolution fully as significant as that launched by Karl Barth more than four decades ago. The incomplete but highly

TOWARD A RELIGIONLESS CHURCH FOR A SECULAR WORLD

suggestive thrusts of Dietrich Bonhoeffer, Hans Hoekendijk, and Harvey Cox form the basis for a radically new understanding of Christianity in the midst of a secular society.

It is against the backdrop of this revolution and the renewal stalemate that I want to trace and test the experience of a single congregation. For the better part of a decade it has been my burden and challenge to work out my understanding of the Church in the midst of the complex metropolitan setting of New York City with a group of people known as the Judson Memorial Church (American Baptist and United Church of Christ). Though Judson has suffered from overexposure in the public press, we have steadily resisted the temptation to write of the church and its pilgrimage from the inside. It is only because I believe Judson's experience may shed some light on present discussions of church structure that I suppress my better judgment and attempt to share the following interpretation.

Judson, located in the midst of New York's Greenwich Village, has been called "an exciting experiment in church life." But it ought to be made clear that the people at Judson (from 1949 when it began its "modern" phase, to the present) never understood themselves as an "experiment". They were simply seeking to learn what it might mean to be a church, obedient and faithful, in the mid-twentieth century in a highly urbanized setting. Judson was never as exciting or faithful as its devotees claimed, nor as "far out" and "radical" as its detractors insisted it was. While one can never be completely objective when one is involved, I think the Judson experience, since 1950 when I was ordained there, can be divided into three phases.

In 1949 Judson was a dirty, yellow pile of stones (*a la* Stanford White) that was rented out to the community for bazaars, dog shows and Police Athletic League jamborees. Spiritually the church existed in the faded glory of a once-proud ministry to neighborhood Italo-Americans—only the skeleton of traditional church organization remained. The lone institutional asset was a modest endowment; the only spiritual asset was that the corpse of the past was all but buried.

The first period—about five years—was marked by a *discovery of the past and a recovery of identity*. The ministers and a small handful of lay persons found themselves engaged in a new search for identity. The search had two aims: to determine the orientation of the church to the surrounding community, and to recover a theologically sound worship and liturgy faithful to the heritage of the free church tradition.

The search for identity during this first phase led the people down many paths: a study group on Kierkegaard in a Greenwich Village coffee house; standing in court with a teenage delinquent; sponsoring an exhibit of Rouault's paintings. The search brought vital changes in the life of the congregation.

If any pattern emerged it was one of "institutional self-emptying." Hoekendijk has called this the "kenotic form" of the Church—the Church that empties itself (see Paul's Letter to the Phillipians) so that it can take the shape that will best represent and identify with the human world around it.

Accordingly the people at Judson sacked the Ladies Aid Societies, Youth Fellowships, etc., in order to make room for ministries that would open the congregation to the life of the surrounding community. In this first period the primary inner activity of the Church was the attempt to understand community outreach in the light of Biblical and theological study. The battle cry was "the sovereignty of God over all areas of man's life and a relevant witness to the culture and the community." And the notion of dialogue between the Church and the world became more conscious in the minds of the congregation.

The second period (also about five years in length) was one of consolidation. It might be termed the "apologetic period." Bultman and Tillich were at their height—this was the time of "the Christian faith and art . . . and literature . . . and poetry." The church moved into the artists' studios of the Village with discussions of Dostoevsky, Camus and Koestler; developed its own art gallery; published a literary quarterly called *Exodus;* and moved deeply into the social and political life of Greenwich Village. The people at Judson identified completely with the causes of the community: political reform; the sponsorship of a center for narcotic addicts; defending the right of Sunday afternoon folk singers to hold forth in Washington Square; and fighting for open, integrated housing throughout the Village.

Amid these involvements, the Judson congregation began to understand the meaning of *proexistence*—that the church existed for others but still maintained a consciousness of "going out into the world" to witness to a "style of life" and a "way of faith." "Witness" was the key word in all our comings and goings. It had none of the overtones of revivalism or pietism; we were sophisticated in our evangelism and urbanity marked the forms of our witness. We did not try to get people into the church by devious means or hidden agendas or phony "dialogues."

Our main task was to show how even "the world" vindicated *our* faith and made our religious posture inevitable. We detested Billy Graham and Dr. Peale for the blatancy and irrelevance of their approach—our allies were Camus, Eliot, Sarte, Picasso, Ginsberg, *et al*. We didn't proof-text with the Bible (our non-believing friends never read it); we pointed to plays by Williams, to paintings by Pollack, to a poem by e. e. cummings and these became the hidden harbingers of our Christian theology.

We used the art and literature of the unbelieving world to drive our victims into some corner of existential despair where all answers failed, and then we slipped them God. We showed our friendly enemies how meaningless was everything they did and were—then drove home *the* meaning that made sense of it all.

Now if this is a caricature of our "witness," it serves at least to point to the basis from which we moved toward "engagement" with the world. However, it was precisely in the moving out, the pursuit of the "apologetic task," the witness in the streets, the coffee houses, the bars, the club house, that we learned that the "world" wasn't as we had pictured it.

Everybody in the coffee houses wasn't drunk on despair and wallowing in self-pity; all scientists weren't on their knees with "mea culpas" because they helped invent and perfect the Doomsday machine; all technologists and research men did not tremble with fear at the anticipation of an automated nightmare of existence; all suburbanites were not empty and vacuous "hollow-men" wandering aimlessly through activities in search of an "ultimate" answer. These were stereotypes and mental images created—*ad nauseum*—by a Christendom that believed the world needed it desperately. In a way God deprived us of our "straw men" in order that we might live with reality, risk and exposure, discovering that the "big ace" we had up our sleeves was only a deuce. Perhaps when we are deprived of our theological edge on the unbelieving world we can learn to be human with the rest of our fellow-beings.

The present period of the pilgrimage of our Judson people is hard to talk about because we are in the midst of it. Our theaters (Dance and Poets'), involvement in the civil rights struggle, the growth of the congregation and the development of a cultural and artistic center, are all the products of these latter times. Reading and studying Bonhoeffer, Bishop Robinson, and the Missionary Structure materials has helped us in self-understanding as a church and given us some *tentative* clues as to what directions and emphases seem to be most significant for us. Perhaps they are significant for other churches as well.

The dynamics of the revolution (social and theological) through which we have been passing are so potent that we may be looking ahead to something that has already happened. At any rate here are some of the emphases and directions which seem important for our future:

Abolition of religion. Perhaps it will seem to some that the most radical move in this post-modern world will be to cease to be "religious." Now I think this is true, but if we are completely honest in our talk about the matter we will refuse to play a semantic game. The argument too often runs: Yes! Religion is dead, that is, all religions *but* Christianity which obviously is not a "religion." So with this fallacy of self-exemption we will kill off all "religion" but ours, thus narrowing all the alternatives which believing people may have.

That's too easy. We have to face the fact when we talk about the abolition of religion, be it by Bonhoeffer or Barth, there is included in the anti-religious critique Christianity itself. Both the Old and New Testaments make it very clear that the major obstacle to restoration of authentic piety to the people is usually religion. The prophetic voices as well as the teachings of Christ hold no brief for religion as such, and we need not mourn its abolition. But we do need to know what this means for our own faith and for the Church.

Any process of true secularization means a humanizing of all pretentious theology and false absolutes. It is perfectly clear that the death of religion could mean the death of some churches, if the church's life is conceived of in purely "religious" terms. This becomes a threat to all forms of authority, especially religious authority where, for example, the preacher assumes some sort of *ex-cathedra* status in his homilies or where his theological interpretation claims infallibility.

Taking the world seriously. This means that as a people of the Way we are recognizing that, even if we cannot confess that the "world has come of age," at least it is a helluva lot older and more mature than the Church's paternalistic and pedagogical posture had assumed it to be. Now this new-found and liberating view about "the world" must not lead us into the romantic illusions and presumptions which have guided our thinking about the Church in the past. The demonic and dehumanizing elements of the world come under critical Judgment in the same way as the Church does.

Our task as a people of Faith is to help the world to be itself. I think we are discovering at Judson what Hoekendijk means by the "ex-centeredness of the Church." The Church's real center of interest is *outside* the Church (religiously conceived)—living and looking for those situations in the world that call for loving responsibility, *there* to work out the shape that God's mission will take. "In mission," Hoekendijk has said, "the Church will come closest to being simply a segment of Main Street...; in the esteem of the world it will certainly be the poorest section of it, without form or comeliness, that segment of Main Street divested of all its illusions." It is not the task of the Church to carve a segment of *holy* space out of the world, to guard some piece of sacred "turf" with the help of our Christian gang. Rather it is to help that world and that Street to be what God intended it to be. (For theological shorthand—Paul Lehman's "making and keeping human life human" will do.)

Disappearance of apologetics. The Judson people are learning to live in a world of the withering away of **apologetics**.

We may have to sacrifice the religious pretensions summarized in Dostoevsky's phrase "miracle, mystery, and authority." In a world come only partially of age, we Christians will no longer be able to play a religious "shell game;" we will no longer be able to claim to know where God is (both in action and intent) and thereby always best the unbeliever.

In a world thoroughly secularized, where authority (not only ecclesiastical, but all kinds) is eroded away, it may be that the highly vaunted "kerygma" of recent Protestant thought is simply irrelevant. What is called for now is a "non-kerygmatic posture—a stance on the part of the Christian which deliberately and meticulously surrenders any claim to authority" (Peter Berger). Once again this is related to the *kenotic* metaphor; Jesus Christ emptied himself, that is, He divested Himself of all religious authority. I think we may get a glimpse of what this might mean for a lot of preaching and teaching done by pastors in churches.

The implications of this are, I believe, that we will be enabled to be human to our fellow-beings. The activities of our church are not justified by the need to convert, cajole or change. The witness is no longer burdened by our having to teach or convince those whom we meet. We no longer have to read a religious commercial in every poem or see a "holy vision" in every painting. We can enjoy art for its own revelation of terror or beauty which it brings to our life. We can "swing" with and appreciate jazz without explaining its religious origins or bringing it into our worship, though there may be a place for the latter.

It is enough if there shines through art, in all its forms, the mystery and creativity that brought it into being. Theology, then, is not a weapon to use against agnostics and atheists, but rather a means by which we clarify our own experience. Let no one mourn the passing of Tillich's bridge-building, apologetic theology. It will take its place in the history of Christian theology with Aquinas' "proofs of God" as having been exceedingly meaningful at a particular period. The point is that the "withering away of apologetics" renders even our most sophisticated attempts at evangelism questionable.

Any dynamic understanding of the Church will have to leave room for new forms or parables of church structure. One of the important definitions of the Church that we have learned at Judson is that *the Church is a "happening."* Several years ago our Judson Gallery played host to a number of young *avant garde* artists who were experimenting with some new art forms known as "environments" or "happenings." A happening is "an art form that one enters, submits to, and is, in turn, influenced by." It is fashioned from the real and everyday world—a world it celebrates, probes, and comments upon.

The Church is a real *happening* in the world; it "happens" where we are sure it cannot, and it happens whether men believe it or not. Like grace, a church happening is one of the surprises of God and we seldom can predict it. The church never happens the same way twice and it is shaped tremendously by the people who perform and the space where it takes place.

It is significant that *the Church happens in a space or place.* For some time, during the anti-building kick which accompanied the recovery of the truth that the Church is people, we felt very guilty about our Romanesque, rambling old brickpile. At times we were ashamed not to have sold it and gone "on the road," but as we saw *mission* "happen" here we realized that the church must happen in a place or space. To deny this is to raise a serious question about the reality of the Incarnation. When the Church becomes a reality it is incarnate, visible, concrete, occupying a certain space at a certain time. Hans Schmidt says that the Holy Spirit is never a timeless manifestation.

To illustrate: Remember that in the South it was church *buildings* that were bombed and burnt to the ground! We need not apologize for the building (whether it is irrelevant Gothic or hideous modern) but for what happens there. If the building is only a religious ghetto housing a holy enclave, it won't matter and nobody will bother to burn it or mark obscenities on its doors.

I recall how my mind has changed over the years on this matter. When I first came to Judson I was terribly uneasy about outsiders and non-religious organizations using the main meeting room (sanctuary) of the church. I remember the offense I felt when a political group wanted to put bunting over the cross during a rally there. The irony of my position later became apparent to me: I was preaching involvement and identification with the world but careful to maintain a special, holy place for the Church. My attitude toward the building hadn't caught up with my theology.

The students at Judson's Urban Life Project last summer were much more perceptive on this matter. In discussing worship at Judson, several students spoke of the "familiarity of the space" which was the setting for worship. The week before they had been to a dance concert there, attended a Mississippi freedom rally and had eaten dinner there, so that as they came to offer worship it was a place they knew, where life had been lived, issues faced, and where joy and laughter had filled familiar surroundings. It has a "holiness" all its own, not dependent on its being set aside but on its being a setting for the common concerns and cares of this life.

We've seen buildings become traps and retreats and museums to house religious antiquities and when this happens, mission is denied. But this ought not to lead to what is apparently a denial that faith and obedience are a response to a particular time and place. It is when the Church is everywhere that it is nowhere; it is when the Church is exclusively eternal that it is never timely; it is when the Church is spiritual that it is not material to anyone. A building (whether storefront or cathedral) can be the *space* where the Church happens, the shelter where the thoroughly secularized world can be itself, and where men can care for one another with deep concern.

In all the "renewal talk" of the past fifteen years and the "missionary structures" talk of the last two years, there has been a consistent rumor of the death of the local congregation. All who are dissatisfied with the innocuousness or sickness of the Church hailed the announced demise of the local church as good news. Meanwhile every religious bureaucrat or denominational executive (using the local church as a *raison d'etre* for his position) decried such blasphemy as tantamount to heresy and a denial of God. So the critics of the Church were divided into two camps: the renewers and the revolutionists. Those who believed that it was possible to save the church advocated renewal; they said the only possible salvation was in the purification of the People of God. There was a need, to be sure, for

Toward A Religionless Church For A Secular World

some winnowing of wheat from chaff in order to produce the "real Church." Thus the renewers were able to limit the Church to those who knew what Christian faith was. This core group of committed and devoted persons would form the creative center of a renewal movement that would, in turn, transform the entire Church.

The people at Judson are seeking to rediscover the Church in a somewhat different direction—that of *inclusiveness*. Judson today makes little distinction between "true believers," inquirers, and non-believers. Out of this openness has developed a community of mankind that includes Christians, agnostics, atheists, persons of faith and unfaith. The touchstone of the community is still the Christian gospel (without apology); the metaphysical mood is one of waiting and seeking.

The Christian faith, in so far as it is perceived and communicable, is still held and taught, but only under the most rigorous questioning and probing of the non-believer in our midst. Formal worship is still practiced (albeit with some unease), but it is subject also to ridicule and probing by people who are demanding that symbols mean something, that language say something, that liturgy be alive.

I personally doubt whether our people could have found meaning and significance if it had not been for the unbeliever in our midst, close to the heart of our congregational life.

Perhaps the most misleading term in all this talk of "church structure" has been the term "local congregation" which usually is described as residential and family centered. Someone has suggested that a more fitting term for this is "the biological church." The point is that, at Judson, we have found this community—incarnate and specific—very important. It is, in fact, the indispensable and irreducible quality in the meaning of the Church.

The origin of the gathered community is unimportant whether it develops in the inner city neighborhood, suburbia, or exurbia. What is important is that a community of persons does come together with concern *for* the world, bound in a "messianic pattern" (servanthood, self-denial, humiliation) to each other, and willing to lay organizational life on the line in loving service of the world. This secularized, Christian community deprived of its religious activities, spiritual games, and holy calendars is freed to discover the new shape of mission in terms of human need and the social structures given us by the world. The pilgrimage that has been Judson's experience is fraught with dangers, but what wanderings of God's people were ever without risk and the real possibility of denial of the very Lord we live to serve? □

PART FOUR

NEEDED: AN APPROACH TO THE FUTURE

The following selections are straws in the wind. They look to the future in the light of the present. They are suggestive rather than conclusive. Which way is the wind blowing? And is the Church listening to the wind as it rumbles, whispers, pushes, dances? The wind is nothing less than the Spirit of God. It thrusts us into the now. It asks us to bear towels, hot water, forceps to the countless chambers where the world is continually being born. And, like the Biblical Spirit, the beckonings of the wind are set in the context of the ordinary events of history. Essentially, the pieces that follow deal with leisure and apathy, in other words, with the potential shape of technological society and with the appropriate understanding of sin in an age of affluence. They ask us to form not only new ministries for a new age, but to begin to forge a new consciousness of the meaning of freedom and responsibility. □

Saying Yes To Leisure

By Stephen C. Rose

Within this century, two percent of our population will be able to produce the goods and food needed for the other ninety-eight percent.

For the first time in history, man's environment is within his control.

What the new leisure does is to present man with a vast range of choices about how he will use his time . . . Confronted with an abundance of *anything,* we may become bored with *everything.*

But man's central problem remains unchanged: how to become human in this world . . . Will the generations freed from the work of the past be able to forge a new culture, a new life, a new self-understanding to sustain themselves in the years to come?

(Excerpts from the narration of EDEN, U.S.A., a twenty-five minute film on the new leisure produced by the United Church Board for Homeland Ministries.)

> If all the year were playing holidays,
> To sport would be as tedious as to work.
>
> —William Shakespeare

THE person reading these words may well frown impatiently at the suggestion that we are experiencing a leisure revolution. If he is male, he very likely commutes three hours a day to an eight-hour-a-day job, toys with notions of tranquilizers, and wishes the Church, the local clubs, the endless committee meetings would vanish for long enough to give him a well-earned breather. If the reader is female, the chances are that she has similar problems—a house to keep, children to mind, a full or part-time job, and enough requests to serve on this or that committee to keep her busy for life.

So perhaps the first reaction could be summed up in an ironic, frustrated outburst: "Leisure. Ha! I don't even have any free time!"

Leisure and free time, as both welfare recipients and $15,000-a-year-men know, are two different things. So we can begin by asking whether our society really does provide more free time than, let us say, it did in the late 19th century.

The answer is yes, even when one adds in all the extra commuting hours as the time-price we pay for living in abundant, urbanized America. In the 19th century we had the twelve hour day, the six or seven day work week; we began work earlier in life and the notion of a long "retirement" was reserved for the wealthy. Just as significant is what we did *not* have. We didn't have cars, we didn't have power-mowers, and we had none of the automatic time-saving devices in our homes. One had to wash the laundry by hand; one began preparing supper after breakfast.

Suddenly we realize that if our lives are crowded today, *they are crowded by choice*. The economy demands no more from most of us than a forty-hour week. Most of us have two full days a week when we can do as we please. If we have a job during the day, we have time in the evenings. We *choose* to serve on committees, to attend Church services, to go to the ball-game or bowling alley, to pave a patio, to prepare a recipe instead of a TV dinner. If we have no free time, it is because we have chosen not to have it. And if most of us were deprived of television, the automobile and the endless twentieth century hobbies—from photography to camping to model airplanes—we would go beserk. We fill our time, and we do it voluntarily.

But carry the question a bit further. Someone may say, "Very well, I do what I have to do and there *still* isn't enough time." The answer leaps out like the Hound of Heaven. There will be time, lots of it. Consider the following awesome projection.

The old notion that the rich and prominent have more free time than the lower classes is being reversed. Today we are witnessing the creeping giants of automation and cybernation (the wedding of computers and machines). These twin giants strike first at the jobless—assuring them that even with a rudimentary education there may be little place for them in the labor market of the future. But the giants do not stop there. They tap at the shoulders of middle-echelon white collar workers. "Machines and computers," they whisper, "can do your work more efficiently, more economically, than you can." Are they friendly giants or not? Regardless of your answer, the estimate is that Americans will have over 600 *billion* more hours of free time in the year 2,000 than they now have. Machines and computers will eliminate the need for most semi-skilled workers (from typesetters to stenographers to junior accountants) not to mention the factory laborers who could be replaced *even today* at considerable savings to the companies involved. There will be jobs for teachers, doctors, and other professionals. Business will need men to manage the machines. Wives will still have to push the right buttons and diaper their infant children. But, yes, there will be more free time than our grandparents ever dreamed of. Workers used to strike to gain a shorter work week. Today we can envision unions fighting to maintain the right to work. The sheer abundance of free time will be experienced mostly by our children and by *their* children. But the decisions we make will be the key, in many ways, to the choices they will have.

But free time is not leisure. It is merely a framework in which leisure is possible. Let us first suggest what leisure is *not*. Leisure is *not* one activity as opposed to another. It is not painting a picture as opposed to bowling. It is not listening to a symphony as opposed to a rock-and-roll record. We cannot define leisure by listing a series of pursuits that we feel will be *rewarding*. Such a definition of leisure would be snobbish and narrow in the extreme. It assumes that leisure exists outside of one's attitude about what one does.

In addition, leisure is *not* the opposite of work. In many ways, the leisure revolution is as relevant to the world of the job, the occupation, as it is to the world of free time. For, in the deepest sense, leisure is whatever involves us, excites us, and brings out our interests and abilities; leisure exists only to the extent that we are *freely engaged* in what we are doing. As suggested above, the only available jobs in the years to come will be jobs that we *choose*. Most of the busywork, the impersonal assemblyline labor, the uncreative bureaucratic treadmill, could be eliminated. So even as we *choose* what we do in our free time, we shall choose what we do to make a living.

What then is leisure? It is the free engagement of the individual with whatever moves him toward self-realization. When Adam was expelled from Eden, he was ordered to work by the sweat of his brow. But Adam, Man, was more than a drone. He was fallen man, but man nonetheless. And the entire Bible bears witness to this dual nature of man. He moves between rebellion and obedience, slavery and freedom, degradation and victory. The supreme revelation of God—the God-man Jesus Christ—is the prototype of freedom, obedience and victory. Through Him, man is liberated from the curse that falls upon Adam. The traces of the curse remain. But the chains of slavery are broken.

So leisure, for the Christian, becomes a question of attitude—toward oneself, toward one's neighbor, toward God. Are we to be men or piano keys? Do we accept the world of slavery? Or do we embrace our freedom . . . to create, to exist fully, to love? Our answer to this question defines our attitude toward life. Drudgery remains, of course, and the world where people still are broken and hungry is surely no paradise. But it is our world and the word of Genesis is that we are to be masters of the creation, even as the artist is the master of his materials. And the word of the New Testament is that we are given new life, life which liberates us to enjoy God's graciousness.

So do we dance joyously like Zorba the Greek, taking no thought for the morrow, or do we fearfully seek refuge in a cloak of inhibition where life is merely a hollow procession of spiritless escapes from real engagement?

Free time exists. It will increase. But the question of whether leisure exists is addressed directly to each individual. For it is the person who must determine whether what he or she does points to free engagement and self-realization or to something else, boredom perhaps or fear or involuntary servitude.

Soon, however, we realize that what we have said is too simple. Yes, there's free time. Yes, leisure is a matter of inner attitude. But can anything approaching leisure exist in the environment we are creating for ourselves? Some few may escape to the mountain top where horns don't blare and where the work of one's own hands is necessary for the preservation of one's own life. But the rest of us are metropolitan. Our freedom is limited. If we are masters of creation, we are also objects of enslavement. We involve ourselves in everything and find that we are involved in nothing. Even if we are truly inner-directed, leisure is almost impossible in this era of high blood pressure, congested highways, and perpetual TV. Are there adequate facilities today, not only for recreation, but for *re-creation*, for the renewal of one's inner being?

In the film EDEN, U.S.A., beyond the glimpse we get of Leisure City, Florida, beyond montages of modern appliances and roadside billboards, there is a brief, but pointed, sequence: The camera zooms back to reveal a panoramic vision of a medium-sized city—a symbol of the metropolis that we are designing. Human attitudes are reflected in the buildings we build, the streets we plan, the way we zone land for parks, factories and houses. Where, in the new metropolis, is the space, the environment, that *frees* man? Where is the imagination, the daring, the willingness to recognize a need for diversity? Where is the environmental recognition of man's need for adventure? In the ticky tacky split levels, row upon row? Perhaps, for the human spirit is not solely dependent on environment. In the way we transport ourselves, amid exhaust fumes and bumper to bumper traffic? Perhaps, for man can transcend traffic jams on occasion. But one is led to ask whether the ultimate expression of American culture is to be the jukebox beside the superhighway. Or can abundance free men and women to set higher sights, not only for themselves, but also for the quality of the space in which they live?

Can leisure exist? Again each person must judge for himself. To what extent does our physical environment limit expression of who we are, of who we might be?

We have more time today. We have the technical capacity to control our environment. So we can phrase our two original questions (Does leisure exist? Can leisure exist?) in a blunt and crucial form: Will leisure exist?

It seems a harmless question. But it carrys with it a burden of urgency. The answer is inevitable: *Leisure must exist*. Remember the definition of leisure as a capacity for self-realization, for creative involvement, for freedom.

Will leisure exist? If the answer is no, consider the implications. We shall have to find a way to occupy the vast majority of the population without the traditional time-filler of hard labor. The alternative to leisure might well be the mass distribution of tranquilizers to dull the nation's fear of the awesome weight of unfilled hours. Along with this, there would have to be a refinement and expansion of radio and television so that scarcely a moment would pass without some diversion to remove from man's mind the suspicion that he is a man rather than a piano key. Some totalitarian government, a George Orwell, *1984,* incarnation of Big Brother, might succeed in producing a new slavery. Instead of real work, there could be make-believe work. We would become like the captured squirrels in their circular mesh cages, who run constantly, and yet remain stationary. In short, we would find a way to fill our time and, simultaneously, to avoid leisure.

This is the era of science fiction come true, so we would be remiss if we neglected a second alternative. Perhaps, eventually, man's scientific capacities will enable him to find a new form of work—the colonization of space. Here, indeed, would be a challenge equal to the thirst for self-realization. But that is possibly one hundred years in the future. It may serve the adventurous instincts of our grandchildren.

The third alternative is as depressing as the first and as possible as the second. It is the *possibility* (we know it deep inside if we do not admit it in discussion) that we would prefer self-destruction to a serious reckoning with the implication of the new leisure. We might saturate ourselves in Big Brother's Elixir of Endless Disengagement for a time, and seeing no alternative, generate the psychological adrenalin needed to push the final button. Having been given control of the creation and allowed the creation to control us, we could perhaps accept extinction. Better that than endless boredom, prepackaged life, and the absence of choice. So, someday, we might feel.

So leisure *must* exist, if the new world is to be born, if it is to survive its cataclysmic infancy.

The Church adapted well to the burden laid upon Adam. It propounded a theology of work. In America that theology—the so-called Protestant ethic—reached the pinnacle of refinement. Salvation itself lay in work. The better one did, the more salvation there was. And the nation was built. Then, irony of ironies, the very notion of hard work as the seal and sign of divine favor, produced a nation where work—in the old sense—is less and less necessary. Now the Church must forge a new theology based on a new reality.

Christian obedience must be seen as responsible *management* of the machines and computers that make traditional work obsolete.

The Church will have to recognize that joblessness (unemployment) is not, in itself, a mortal sin. Today we look upon the unemployed as irresponsible persons. Tomorrow we shall have to redefine employment in terms of what one does with one's time, whether or not this turns out to be work in the traditional sense.

In an abundant society the rewards of work will be different. If jobs themselves are scarce, financial rewards will be less important than the jobs themselves. People will work because they want to, and only secondarily because they have to. And in this sense, work will take on the qualities of leisure. It will represent the free engagement of the individual with what interests him.

Theoretically, a society might emerge in which everybody would have a basic income and in which additional rewards would be given to individuals who elected to make a contribution to the culture in a number of service areas—ranging from what we now call professions to what we now consider free-time activities.

In optimistic moments, we can say that the new technology is part of God's graciousness, for it gives us the means by which we can spread abundance to nations where poverty is the rule. But, as with pockets of poverty in America, we know that mere abundance without the means of responsibly using it, is as deadly as poverty itself. The machines we have built will either make possible a twenty minute war, or the time to create peace.

At the outset we quoted Shakespeare's lines:

> If all the year were playing holidays,
> To sport would be as tedious as to work.

The words are wise because they tell us what we deeply sense: that if our free time is invested with no greater meaning than our traditional work time, we shall live, if at all, with tedium. But the words are cynical too, for they foreclose the possibility of new visions. The idea of leisure, shorn of all Puritanical notions of laziness and idleness, is the vehicle of a new vision for society. It enables us to accept the challenge of free time. It pushes us to realize our responsibility for our environment. And, most important, it suggests a viable shape for future generations. If there is no leisure, there is only *1984* or the void.

Inevitably, someone will ask, "What can we do?" As Will D. Campbell pointed out several years ago, the more appropriate question is, "What can we be?" Words will not provide the only answer. "What we can be" can only be determined by doing and being. Perhaps we will take our deepest dreams and make them come to life. Perhaps we will be less afraid of empty hours, having been told that we are free to decide for ourselves what their use shall be. For the time is coming when the magic question, "If you could do anything in the world, what would you do?" will not be fantasy for us, but fact. □

The Uses of Leisure Time
By Robert Spike

ONE remembers with amazement that it was only thirty years ago that the life of a farmer and his wife began at 5:30 every morning of the week and ended with exhaustion at nine in the evening by falling like a log into bed.

We live in a different world as far as the rhythm of work, worship and leisure is concerned. One of the major facets of the life of the mid-twentieth century is the leisure revolution. It well may be the most significant aspect of the affluent industrial culture we now enjoy as far as the goals and driving forces of our society are concerned. We all know it is in the present, and yet it is difficult for us to visualize its impact on the next half century.

The twenty hour week for great masses of people is just around the corner. The churches and other institutions of the social fabric may be slow to recognize it, and yet commercial interests have not been slow. Vast fortunes have been made out of the new leisure market, from Brunswick bowling equipment to numerous boat companies. The great blanket of the entertainment industries is so smothering that we almost fail to recognize its existence.

There are times when I think of Las Vegas, Nevada as a frightening vision of our future civilization. Here is a whole city harnessed to the entertainment industry, and I can't stand to be there more than 24 hours at a time—not because of the gambling alone but because of the dreary emptiness of such a life.

There are many implications for the life of the Christian and the Christian community. Let us isolate just a few.

First, it may be necessary to *rethink the doctrine of man's calling,* this very keystone of our historic Calvinist theology. For the doctrine of the sovereignty of God, His mighty acts in history and His grace all impinged ultimately on the question, "What do you do about it—what is your response in the world?" Thus the importance of a man's employment was placed alongside his own personal piety as the very substance of Protestant religion. Accompanying this was the ingrained distrust of enjoyment of leisure in the Puritan world view which leaves us badly prepared for handling leisure. Thus faced with great quantities of it, we turn to mass narcosis. We use TV as a sleeping tablet. We try to escape like little children. The doctrine of calling has yet to be re-thought and re-presented to people to include the gift of leisure.

It may also be necessary to *re-examine radically the calling of the Church*.

1. *First in the local congregation*. Its life becomes lost in a sea of competitive efforts to fill leisure time. There is no one convincing prescription here.

On the one hand, stripping church program to the essentials seems imperative, so that we are not running second rate county fairs, Athenaeums and Lions Clubs—so that the celebration of worship, directly, clearly, corporately, is really central. It may mean giving up Sunday morning as the one set aside time when this happens.

But, in another way of looking at it, the uses of leisure are now so awkward, so trivial, that one urges the Church to move heavily into the adult education field. This is not a universal recommendation but in many instances, through small groups and drama, for example, a whole new stewardship of life can be developed. The maturing of Christian discrimination and taste in art and culture may be the most important preparation a church can give its people as moulders and consumers of a mass society. Through this teaching ministry, in imagination and otherwise, the word is really broken open. Here may be the locus of the prophetic ministry.

2. But beyond the restructuring of the life of the local congregation there is another concern—we must outgrow our continual insistence that the normative expression of the Church's life is the local residential parish. Coupled with the great mobility of our population, I am afraid that new patterns of leisure will create a situation in which Protestantism will be caught off in a side eddy if it continues to rely on the residential parish as the only place where the gospel is preached, where the Christian evangel is carried on.

I am *not* forecasting the abandonment of the parish church, but only wish to alert us all that we cannot concentrate there as the only place of ministry to a moving, leisurely people.

That is why we must develop a whole battery of specialized ministries of all kinds, as a part of the cooperative ministry of the church as a whole. We must do this vocationally but also in places where people are at leisure, weekends, summers and holidays.

What I do see is a new mission field as drastic and bewildering as the land beyond the Mississippi a century ago, or the city slum a half century ago. We must interpret this to our people—their involvement in it and also the need to support ministries that will serve people where they are at leisure, at play, in the mass leisure market of TV, drama and publications. □

Experiment: Chicago's "Door"

By Bill Southwick

THE young people come to Chicago—not because it's new, not because it's old but because it's here, and this is where you find the jobs, the girls, the boys, and before long the loneliness. The growing up years were in Lincoln, Neb., or Peotone, Iowa. Four years of college happened in Madison or Indianapolis. The young people come to work as secretaries, IBM operators, nurses and the nights are spent with questions in one room apartments.

The old timers and some of the newcomers have lived through or heard about the coffee house tradition of Chicago. There were places where people talked, and argued, and fought philosophy or politics. There was the Dill Pickle. There was the College of Complexes. There were places where you ducked your head and left your dignity behind. But now the talkers wander lonely streets or eat in cafeterias hoping for someone to listen, and searching for that rare moment when someone agrees.

Look closely at these two kinds of wandering young adults, and then go to a service some Sunday in one of the churches on Chicago's north side. Note the average age of the congregation. You might see two twenty year olds; you might see one thirty year old. You might be lucky.

In 1963 the North Side Co-operative Ministry began to see these young wanderers around them. The statistics had pointed them out, but several of the ministers knew some of them. The Ministry felt the need to go into this world. The Ministry felt the need to go into this wandering world to listen and to make known a bias—the Christian bias.

The Ministry, which had just organized itself from 24 struggling inner-city churches, could afford nothing, but they listened carefully and took an honest leap of faith. On Nov. 19, 1963, they opened a coffee-house and called it The Door. They had a few things to go on—there had been other Church coffee-houses in this country—but this was a different neighborhood, and different people. The first month or so was a real struggle, but after the new year the people came—the secretary from Peotone and the talker from Bug-House Square.

We varied our program to meet the needs of many people. On Tuesday nights we ran an open forum discussion. A topic was picked and everyone was invited to make a speech or ask a question. We heard the thoughts running through many minds—anarchist thoughts, Christian thoughts, and conservative thoughts.

We kept Wednesday and Thursday nights free of programs. These were times for quiet talking and sharing of concerns and hopes. On many nights we heard that the Church was a fake, or that Christ was an honest man, or that the Gospel is good news.

On Friday nights the folksingers arrived. Young amateurs who had walked from the Loop with guitar on backs. They sang "Times they are a'changin'" and "If I had a Hammer." Some were honest songs, and we could listen.

The Door was now a place—a place to listen and a place to speak, a place to break down and a place to build up. The Door was staffed by volunteer workers from local churches who arrived one night every two weeks to serve coffee, wash dishes and to minister. They were people committed to the Word they had heard spoken and to the demand to be real in the world. They met new people and sometimes strange people. The workers began to grow in their involvement with the lonely. They found that they were speaking in a new tongue and they were being given this tongue. The Door was not becoming a separate congregation for them but they continually felt the need to be driven anew by the Word into this situation.

We all saw things, and were convinced that something was happening here that would not have happened either in a Church basement or in the bar across the street.

The night before Easter a young addict who had been on dope for twelve years came in to say that he wanted to "kick the habit." We waited through a midnight mass in a Catholic church on the South Side to hear of the one great triumph and to talk to a priest who could get our friend into a clinic.

A Spinoza-reading cab driver who had spent many years alone headed home one night and said: "thank you for the Door."

Many such things have happened during the last year, but they depended on courage at many points. It depends on courageous ministers speaking the Word in truth, for this true word sends people into the world. It demands courageous workers who are willing to take a boy with a beard seriously. It demanded a courageous sensitivity and willingness to speak the truth in love. And it demands time to get involved, time to listen, and time to wash dishes.

During the year we have simply attempted to live in the leisure world of the young adult, listening and speaking. We did not go into this with the idea of getting anything in return by way of converts or enlarged church memberships or community utopias, but we have been given a commission to look for God's activity in all, even the strange places of the world. Perhaps this is the greatest gift we could have received.

We have had our share or difficulties. There have been financial crises even though we have paid our running expenses. There have been times when we said the wrong things. There have been times when people have not understood what we were doing. But new things still happen at the Door.

Two small study groups have begun to discuss theological books in depth. They meet once a week in people's apartments around the North Side. In these groups a spirit of sharing has been a real fact.

A person is beginning to spend some time in the homosexual bars in the neighborhood. He is trying first of all to understand the problems of this sub-culture, and then to see how the church might work in this area.

We have opened on Sunday afternoons, and during this time watch the TV program "Profiles in Courage." The discussion about the program goes on long after we close. It has been a good year in which we feel that we have ministered to people and in which we have been ministered unto.

We do not feel that the Door is the *only* type of ministry, that this is the *only* kind of thing that should be done. But we feel that the Door has been something more than an "experiment"—it has been an experience in listening to the Word of God from strange mouths and speaking the same Word in a new tongue. □

Freedom Now!

By Stephen C. Rose

THIS is rightfully the cry of American Negroes who are seeking to break the shackles of white oppression, but not exclusively so. *Freedom* is an elusive term and *now* has many meanings. The terms—used in a different context—have an urgency that knows no color or class. Freedom, not in the sense of the right to vote or drive a car. Now, but not in the sense of "right now". Think of freedom as a deep, profound, personal sense of inner release. Consider freedom less as a right than a quality of life. How many are there who enjoy every advantage and right save the only one that matters: the inner capacity to reach out, to touch, to listen, to see, to enjoy, to participate. The opposite of freedom, in this sense, is inhibition, pettiness, narrowness. The lack of such freedom is the most persistent characteristic of residents of the land of the free and the home of the brave. It is not the only freedom, to be sure, but it is a level of freedom that is missed in the political orations, speeches, and sermons we hear.

And the now. This may be the exclamation of a mother chiding a procrastinating child. "Now!" But the term also refers to the ability to live in the present, to grasp the moment with passion and perception. To live in the now is a lost art of Americans, with their constant thinking of the past and general preoccupation with the future. We have the cocktail party as the symbol of having a good time in our society, but the cocktail party smacks more of frantic running to and fro than of unreserved enjoyment and present communication.

To live with freedom in the now—this epitomizes the goal of the artist. Without such freedom discipline is impossible, human relations are hollow, and all the other freedoms are like the unused toys piled in the affluent closets of ungrateful children.

Such freedom is a gift: it cannot be conjured up by determination or effort alone. Some have it; they are known—some for graciousness, some for exceptional courage, some for humor, some for creative works that fill galleries. Often such freedom is given to those who have stood on the brink of extreme mental illness or physical death. Others are given a talent or vocation which releases creative energies in such abundance that they spill over in an outpouring of giving to others. This freedom is not absolute or untainted. It dwells in those who acknowledge deep fears, and in those whose lives are characterized by weakness. It is out of such freedom that lives are sustained, cultures created, forgiveness mediated.

In a society clutched by fear, the predominant attitude will be one of withholding . . . the very opposite of freedom. The late Roman Empire knew such fear. Is this our fear? That there is no time, no real possibility of life, no enjoyment save the mass-produced insulation that calls itself pleasure?

The free person hates racial segregation not only because it is unjust, but because it is ugly. He hates war not simply because the numerical tally of the prospective dead is incalculable, but because war is an offense against dignity and beauty. He hates mass produced dwellings because they are unimaginative children of someone's backfiring financial wizardry.

For free men and women, such phrases as the sacredness of the individual and the sanctity of the imagination will be more than cliches. For them parables are more meaningful than laws, illustrations more helpful than rules.

Such thoughts, it seems to me, begin to point to the function of the artist—whether painter or humorist or dancer or writer or mathematician or actor. Theirs is the task of articulating the laughter and tears that circumscribe the globe in which we invest so much frenetic worry.

Aesthetics will not replace ethics, but aesthetics can laugh at the cold pomposity of the moralist. It may even say to the ardent pursuers of justice, and to the pursued, "What difference will it all make? What is this freedom of which you speak?" □

Apathy, Abdication, and Acedia
By Harvey Cox

TRYING to relate modern apathy to the Biblical doctrine of sin is no easy task. Sin is not a popular theological subject today and when it comes to teaching us what it is really all about, our two best instructors in recent years have not been theologians, but Hannah Arendt and James Baldwin. Arendt's portrait of Adolph Eichmann, subtitled "A Study in the Banality of Evil," despite some justifiable criticisms made of it, remains a graphic portrayal of sin in the twentieth century—monstrous crimes perpetrated by insipid sad-sacks. It terrifies us because Eichmann is so overpoweringly ordinary, so like us. As his featureless face gradually takes form in Arendt's pages he is disclosed as the kind of spectacle-polishing milquetoast with whom we would be bored after ten minutes if we had to sit next to him on a commuter train. Yet it is Eichmann's vapid triteness which reflects our own sin. Incapable of Luciferian evil, we could all commit genocide just by getting to work on time and keeping our noses clean.

If Arendt dismantles our prevailing images of sin by introducing us to the dolt-as-deathmonger, Baldwin performs the same service inversely by seeing in the Negro militant the saint-as-revolutionary. Others have used such an image before, especially Arthur Koestler and Ignazio Silone. But they were both too European in their mentality to speak to many Americans. Baldwin gets to us because he opens our eyes to the saints among us. And they are not the other-wordly, self-effacing saints of the religious bookstores but angry hotheads, impetuous activists impatiently persuing social change and spiritual wholeness. In providing us with a new model of religious obedience, Baldwin has also exposed the criminal sinfulness of our law-abiding complacency and inactivity.

The sharpened awareness of sin which Baldwin and Arendt have brought us catches Christian theologians at an embarrassing time. The truth is that the ideas of sin with which we are now working are probably more Greek than Biblical, and not even very good Greek at that. The word "sin" itself has lurid, titillating and tempting overtones. It suggests sentimentality and cultural repressions thinly coated with pictures of Adam and Eve and a superbly phallic serpent.

Admittedly theologians have been working for some years now to repair the damages done to Christian theology by the uncritical importation of Greek categories. Work is proceeding apace on historical theologies and secular ethics. God has *almost* become a Hebrew again. But in the meantime our images of man remain largely Greek, or more precisely, Promethean.

The process goes as follows: Pride is rightly seen as the basic element of man's sin; but then pride is mistakenly identified with rebelliousness and man-the-sinner is wrongly pictured as the fist-shaking, contemptuous insurrectionary. He is seen as the creature who "doesn't know his place," who storms the heavens with such audacity that God must constantly summon the host to quell the revolt. This basically Greek image, larded here and there with the cautionary warnings of bourgeois culture, has persisted in diverting our attention from the main thrust of the Bible for centuries. The result in western literature has been a none-too-secret admiration for man as the heroic sinner. Projected mythologically we find Lucifer and Satan, whether in Goethe or in Milton, far more interesting than anyone else. While officially condemning them to flames, we secretly admire them. This distorted image of the sinner-as-rebel has become so deeply lodged in the western mentality that in our own day Emil Brunner *(Man in Revolt)* and Albert Camus *(The Rebel)* both agree that the rebellious human spirit must, by definition, be anti-Christian. Needless to say the former condemns such a spirit while the latter celebrates it.

We need to make a whole new start in reformulating a Biblical doctrine of sin which makes sense of a modern world, with its dutifully compliant Eichmann's and its law-breaking Martin Luther King's, and is at the same time closer to the Bible than the one we have now.

Let us suggest that the ancient and venerable term *sloth* may help us in this undertaking. Sloth means being *less* than, not more than, man. Sloth means the determined or lackadaisical refusal to live up to one's essential humanity. It is the torpid unwillingness to revel in the delights or to share in the responsibilities of being fully human. It means to decline a full share of that characteristic life-with-life which *is* human existence in the world.

"Sloth" is the English word we use to translate the Latin word *acedia* which is derived in turn from the Greek words "not caring" (*a*—not; *kedos*—care). The Church Fathers listed sloth (along with pride, covetousness, lust, anger, gluttony and envy) as one of the seven deadly, or capital sins. Calvin emphasized sloth heavily, but the later Calvinist theologians associated it too closely with the bourgeois-capitalist vice of laziness or lack of ambition. Theologians have generally conceded that both pride and sloth played an important role in man's sin, that the two are in some sense inextricable. Why then has pride, seen almost always as rebellion, been so overemphasized while sloth *(acedia)* has been nearly forgotten?

One reason is that we have located the Fall of man too narrowly in the forbidden fruit fable in Genesis. "In Adam's fall we sinned all." And so we did, or do; but modern Biblical scholars indicate that the *whole* first section of Genesis, not just the Adam and Eve story, was intended to illuminate man's fractured relationship to the creation. Thus the stories of Cain and Abel, of Noah and the Ark and of the Tower of Babel are just as important as the Garden of Eden story in symbolizing the character of man's sin. They all concern the ways in which man abdicates his assignment of living in brotherly reciprocity with his fellow man and with the natural order. He is always looking for a way out. Instead of faithfully naming the creatures whom God entrusts to him, cultivating the garden of the earth and enjoying its fruits, exercising dominion over the beasts and living in reciprocity with his fellow man, he sells out.

The first thing he does is to let one of the animals tell him what to do. He surrenders his position of privilege and responsibility. From then on there is nothing but trouble. Pride and sloth then work in tandem to disfigure the world. Thus to read the story of the Fall entirely in terms of defiant pride is to rely on Sophocles rather than the Genesis account, the only difference being that for the Greeks, King Oedipus was in some strange way fulfilling his destiny by defying fate while for the Bible, Adam was frittering away his destiny.

In Adam, the man who at first will not and then can not be man, the Bible sees all men. But with the coming of the

Second Adam, Christ, that changes. Here was a man who would be and was a full man. In him the whole range of human responsibility is fully taken up again. He exercises the full prerogatives of manhood. He lives in vigorous reciprocity with thieves, priests, prostitutes and little children. In the stories that Jesus spins, one of the most frequent characters is the steward, the man who has the responsibility and exercises the power assigned to him by the master. The cautious or irresponsible steward, the one who hides his money in the earth or beats the servants in the master's absence, reaps the rebuke of Jesus. The Apostle Paul also sees the life that God makes possible for man as that of an heir who, putting childhood dependencies firmly behind him, assumes the duties of an adult. *It is thus quite evident that images of timidity, abdication and irresponsibility should figure just as prominently in a Biblical doctrine of sin as do images of rebellion.* Why then has our theological tradition concerned itself so obsessively with insubordination as the chief expression of sin?

Part of the answer can be given in the single word, *politics*. Theologies always develop within a particular political context. There is a political, or perhaps an ideological factor which explains in part why images of protest and revolt became so central in the Christian doctrine of sin. With the conversion of Constantine, Christianity became the ruling ideology of Europe. As such, one of its main functions was to provide the symbolic confirmation of imperial authority and thus to assure the maintenance of social order. It did so with noteworthy success for over a thousand years of relatively unified, western European, "Christian" civilization. It did so by de-emphasizing sloth and accentuating pride as the worst form of sinfulness. Pride of course was equated with insubordination.

When the Reformation came, the magisterial reformers— Luther, Calvin and the Anglicans—largely retained this emphasis. Since they had to rely so heavily on state power for carrying through their programs, they necessarily preserved the dominant image of sinful man as disobedient, fractious and insubordinate. There can be little doubt that the experience these reformers had with the more radical reformers—Muenzer, Servetus, the Levellers—encouraged the *identification of piety with passivity* in their own minds.

By the nineteenth century the merging of faith and docility had become so axiomatic that Kierkegaard, Marx and Nietzsche all had to become enemies of Christendom to make themselves heard. Each was condemned by the church but each was right in his own way. Kierkegaard taught that the only real sin was "the despairing refusal to be one's self"; Marx railed rightly against people who saw society as an eternal "given" rather than as something for which man himself is responsible. Nietzsche saw correctly that a vampire God who will not allow man to be a creator must be killed, and gladly performed that act of deicide himself. Each represents repentance from the sin of sloth at a different level. For Kierkegaard, and for those contemporary existentialists who are most influenced by him, the individual must choose his own identity and not allow himself to be named by the images and expectations others inflict upon him. For Marx, man had to discard his superstitious reverence for unjust social structures before he could begin to change them. Nietzsche hoped for a new man beyond the bourgeois clod of the 19th century, a man who would have the courage to shape the very symbols and meaning by which he would live in the world.

The sin against which these three nineteenth century prophets preached is what classical theologians once called *acedia*, sloth. It is the spiritual paraplegia of modern metropolis.

Sloth is one of the seven "deadly," or more correctly, "capital" sins. This doesn't just mean it is quantitatively worse, but that it is a "source sin," the kind of structural derangement from which other sins arise. As Roman Catholic theologian Joseph Pieper remarks, sloth does not mean mere idleness, as though hyper-thyroid activism were its antidote; rather it means that man "renounces the claim implicit in his human dignity." (*Leisure, The Basis of Culture*, p. 38). In medieval terms this means that the slothful man does not will his own being, does not wish to be what he fundamentally and really is. This is why sloth is such a dangerously fertile sin. It tempts man to other expressions of inhumanity. It leads toward what we might today call estrangement.

God through history summons man to affirm and celebrate what God wants him to be: Man, with all that implies. As Kierkegaard, Marx and Nietzsche saw, to be a man involves personal, social and cultural initiative and responsibility. It means accepting the terrifying duty of deciding *who I will be* rather than merely introjecting the stereotypes that others assign to me. It means opening my eyes to the way power is distributed and wielded in a society and assuming a full measure of pain and temptation that goes with wielding it. It means defying any image of life which discourages criticism or undercuts human creativity. Metaphors which are allowed to become metaphysical become monsters. To be a man means to care for and name the fellow man Eve and with her to have dominion over the earth, to name and care for the creature whom God places in the human world of freedom. To weasel out of any of these privileges is to commit the sin of *acedia*, to relapse into sloth.

All this suggests that apathy is the key form of sin in today's world. Apathy is one of the words Webster uses to define *acedia*. For Adam and Eve, apathy meant letting a snake tell them what to do. It meant abdicating what theologians have called the *gubernatio mundi,* the exercise of dominion and control over the world. For us it means allowing others to dictate the identities with which we live out our lives. Sartre's portrait of Jean Genet in *Saint Genet* depicts a man whose view of himself is totally dictated by the mean lusts and foul passions projected on him by others. The Jew, the Negro, the homosexual and the beatnik in our society have sometimes been forced to enact some of these roles for us. But in projecting our secret fears and fantasies onto them we both improverish ourselves and prostitute them. Man is that creature who is created and called by God to shape and enact his own destiny. Whenever he relinquishes that privilege to someone else, he ceases to be a man. It is precisely that Negro who takes off the Sambo costume, who stops playing the humiliating role whites have pasted together for him, who thus affirms the promise of the New Adam. His decision to be himself is an act of repentance from sloth.

But apathy is also, and perhaps mainly a political trespass. It takes the form of hiding behind a specialty, a lack of knowledge, a fear of involvement, which become rationalizations for not assuming one's share in the responsible use of power in the world. Man's existence is, by its very nature, life with and for the fellow man. This makes it essentially political. The apathetic avoidance of politics is the sophisticated way in which we, like Cain, club our brothers to death. We abdicate our assignment as stewards, becoming what C. Wright Mills once called "inactionaries." From the slum Negro who doesn't vote or picket to the MIT scientist who lets Washington decide what shall be done with the weapons systems he is designing, to slough off the political life is to fall into the deadly sin of *acedia,* from which all sorts of lesser venial sins sprout and grow.

We must be careful today with all of our emphasis on the servant role of the church not to give the impression that the call of the Gospel is to plebian servility. It is a call to adult stewardship, to originality, inventiveness and the governance of the world. Let's not let any snake tell us what to do. □

PART FIVE
POSTSCRIPTS, BIASES AND SUNDRY OBSERVATIONS

This is the day that the Lord hath made. Let's rejoice and be glad in it. Such an affirmation can be made only when we've walked through the muck and mire of the public sins that beset our society and when we have confronted the depths of tragedy in our own existence. What follows are some concluding observations. The first, having to do with the Church and race relations, is a small attempt to communicate the difference between the scandalous Gospel and a purely humanistic approach to the critical social issue of our time. If the distinction seems whimsical or unreal, we refuse to apologize for making it. The second is a mulligan stew of proposals and strategies that might bring some animation into the life of the Church. A renewal movement has to emerge. The reader is welcome to join. If the invitation is truly blowing in the wind, if it is the utterance of the Spirit of the confounding personal God of the Old and New Testaments, well and good. We shall rejoice. If we are merely barking up another tree of futility, if our cries echo in the void, then we simply hope you've enjoyed this book. Maybe we'll get together some day despite ourselves. ☐

Whither The Gospel in Race Relations?

By Stephen C. Rose

EVER since Birmingham bombings and Mississippi slayings began to convince America that the Negro might be serious in his demand for equal rights, clergymen have been saying that the response of Christians to the crisis would dictate whether or not the Church was truly relevant in our age.

As events in Birmingham and elsewhere were heralding "the racial revolution of 1963," church groups began to organize in a sort of last ditch effort to prove that they could overcome the lily-white, Anglo-Saxon image of American Protestantism. Numerous religion-and-race groups emerged after the historic Conference on Religion and Race was held in Chicago in January, 1963. Protestant denominations began to organize semi-official groups to meet the problem. And the National Council of Churches cut through the tangle of red tape that afflicts the ecclesiastical bureaucracy to create its Special Commission on Religion and Race, an agency that has done much to mobilize church action on the race issue.

Despite the fact that these moves were made a decade after the 1954 Supreme Court ruling on schools and a full century after the Civil War, the beginnings of Protestant participation in the race struggle seemed laudable.

It can even be said that the churches have proved themselves relevant in the struggle. The President has received the upper echelons of Protestant leadership. And few are the pro-civil rights politicians that fail to praise the Christian community for its concern.

If this is so, then a chorus of praise might be expected from those who contend the renewal of the church depends on a response to the race crisis. But one who listens to the chorus hears a harsh counterpoint. On one side there are those, including most top Protestant leaders, who insist that the churches have "come of age." When Dr. Eugene Carson Blake faced arrest in a Baltimore amusement park in 1963, *Presbyterian Life* magazine wrote of the incident as if the millenium had arrived. Indeed, the mere fact of participation in the struggle was probably enough to convince many Protestant publicists that relevance had finally been attained.

But the other side of the chorus, much smaller in size, is raising insistent questions, questions that must be answered if Protestants are to come to grips with the whole meaning of America's racial upheaval. Does the Church really understand its mission in race relations in a Christian context, or is it jumping on a secular bandwagon in the hope of saving face? Are Christians understanding the race problem in Biblical terms, or are they resting their case for equality on arguments that are no different from the arguments of a good citizen who does not share the Christian faith? Does the Church have a right to criticize society without putting its own house in order?

The man who has pressed questions such as these farther than many of his associates would wish is the Rev. Will D. Campbell, Director of the Committee of Southern Churchmen. His story should illuminate the question of the role of the Church in the race struggle.

Campbell is a white man. He was born to life on a 67-acre cotton farm in a Mississippi town bearing the incongruous name Liberty. During Depression days, in mid-childhood, Campbell received an early lesson in race relations. He and his playmates taunted a colored passer-by with the hated epithet, "nigger." His grandfather told them: "All the niggers are dead, there are only colored people now." But when Campbell grew up to become a minister who led Negro children to school in Little Rock, he alienated the people back home. Now he can feel no righteous sense of rebellion at having shunned the South's traditional racial attitudes because he knows there are members of his family and others throughout the South who are in a tragic position. They see the writing on the wall. They eat their guts out over the problem. But they cannot change.

What is guilt for the white "liberal" in the South? Isn't it departing from the accepted norm? Does not the white Southerner praying for racial justice also secretly petition: "Father, forgive me for not being a segregationist?" Without this insight, the liberal who journeys from the segregated cities of the North to liberate the South just does not understand. Yet if Campbell had to choose between accepting or rejecting the invasions from the North he would say, in most cases, though not without a trace of irony, "Let them come on."

When he graduated from Yale Divinity School, Campbell took a parish in Louisiana, then became a chaplain at the University of Mississippi. He intended to remain at Ole Miss the rest of his life. He was actually there just slightly more than two years. The story of his short tenure on the Ole Miss campus is instructive.

It became known that a speaker Campbell had invited to appear at a religious emphasis week was a contributor to the NAACP. The University raised a fuss and the engagement was cancelled. Campbell responded by refusing to find a substitute. The religious emphasis week became a week of silent prayer for students who were very much aware of why silence was made necessary. Later, in the summer of 1956, Campbell tried to talk a young Negro Baptist preacher into taking a correspondence course at the University. He invited the light skinned Negro to the campus and the two played a game of ping pong in one of the University buildings. A hostile student called the University's Assistant Registrar who demanded of Campbell, "Was he a nigger?" Campbell replied, "Well, if you can't tell the difference, what difference does it make?"

After that the going became rough. Campbell was investigated by the White Citizens Council and the State Sovereignty Commission. He and his wife received intimidating letters and calls. Someone spiked punch at a reception for incoming students with human waste.

The situation became intolerable and Campbell left to join the National Council of Churches Department of Racial and Cultural Relations as head of its Southern Office in Nashville, Tenn., where he has lived ever since.

It was during his time with the National Council of Churches that Campbell's theological understanding of the race problem began to mature, partly in reaction to the official views of the N.C.C. The Council viewed Campbell more or less as "our man in the South." His function was to keep tabs on the racial situation and "to aid the churches in crystallizing a position of action in the solution of community problems in the South."

Campbell grew to see his role in two ways. He could, by virtue of birth and background, go where Northerners feared to tread and help behind the scenes in the resolution of racial conflicts. This he has done with a finesse that has led the Field Foundation to call him an "indispensible man" in the South.

His second, and for him more important role, was to be a preacher to the Southern churches. The job was not to bully the churches into action (a futile process in most cases), but to convince them that racial justice has to do with the Gospel of Jesus Christ. Nowhere in the nation are people more "religious" than in the South. What they need is honest preaching, not from the treatises of Social Work but from the Bible they have known from childhood.

Campbell summed it up in one of the best books to date on religion and race, his *Race and The Renewal of The Church:* "When a church organization needs personnel in the field of human relations it is inclined to look for effective, skilled social reformers or human engineers, but rarely preachers and prophets. . . . All our human engineering is vain if we miss the unambiguous point that, in the (Christian) message, race is irrelevant. The only relevant point has to do with redemption, not race, class, or caste. . . . It might have been better if the Supreme Court had not ruled favorably on the subject of race. Then we would have been forced to speak, if we spoke at all, from the vantage point of the Christian gospel. We would have been required to say, Thus saith the Lord! Not, Thus saith the law! . . . If all church institutions, colleges and universities, hospitals, secondary and primary schools, camps, assembly grounds, homes for the aged and orphanages were open to all, there would not be very much remaining for society to do."

The point of what Campbell is saying is so simple that it is a mystery to determine why his "preaching" proved an enigma to National Council officials and others. He seems to be saying that it might be well for a Christian involved in race relations to preach to the segregationist (and to integrationists) from the standpoint of the Christian Gospel. Now there may be those who argue that the Christian Gospel is confusing and subject to different interpretations. But Campbell's point is that if one is to work within the Church, then one should be subject to the Church's understanding, regardless of how difficult that might be. For to come to a Christian position on race relations from any other perspective is not to renew the churches but to blatently deny that the Church has anything at all to say.

Besides, Campbell contends with great wisdom that the segregationist, both Northern and Southern, is well equipped to argue the issues on secular grounds. But how can he argue, asks Campbell, when faced with the fact that God in Christ reconciled all men to Himself and that, by definition, there is in Christ neither slave nor free, Jew nor Greek?

An added question: The Christian understands that all men are involved in the network of sin that enmeshes our world. The Negro is no better than the white. But, in forfeiting their distinctive understanding, Christians are forced to identify lock, stock and barrel with the aims and ideology of the civil rights groups, aims often every bit as selfish (whether justified or not) as the aims of the segregationist.

The severing of Campbell's relationship with the National Council was a direct result of his interpretation of his job in terms of preaching rather than social engineering. At the Chicago Conference on Religion and Race, Campbell prepared a speech in which he indicated that Negroes—human nature being equal—were as likely to do violence to whites as *vice versa*. He went on to say that the churches should purify their own theology if they are interested in renewing themselves. Campbell's reference to the evil potentialities of Negroes caused panic among National Council officials who prevailed upon him to eliminate the reference from his address. It was not politic, they felt, to say that Negroes were equally bad in relation to whites, though it was perfectly all right to say they were equally good.

This, among other things, triggered Campbell's resignation from the National Council in the summer of 1963.

When he resigned, Campbell was determined to set up an organization that would mirror his conviction that the race problem should be met with the Christian Gospel rather than a humanistic approach. Before long he had organized a group of Southern ministers and laymen to form The Committee of Southern Churchmen. The Committee, with Campbell as the full time staff member, seeks to do three things. Members are committed to preach the Gospel in the South, offering assistance to Christians who are seeking to break the bonds of a heretical, segregationist religion. The Committee will seek to help deposed clergymen remain in the South as "preachers at large." And Committee members will travel to racial trouble spots to bring aid to church groups caught in the despair of hate and indecision. The aim of the Committee is the renewal of the churches of the South. With members in twelve Southern states it seeks to work within the churches to raise basically one question: What does it mean when we say, "God was in Christ, reconciling the world to Himself?"

What Campbell is saying is relevant to the North, for it is becoming plain that the same attitudes exist there. Ministers may preach on the Bill of Rights and the Constitution and the newspaper headlines, but it is clear that significant renewal will involve self-understanding in the light of the Gospel. And for one who regards the Campbell approach with curiosity and perhaps a feeling that it might be an honest one for the Church to pursue, a good starting task would be to read the following excerpt from the inaugural declaration of the Committee of Southern Churchmen:

> In dying for all men, Christ destroyed every barrier which denies fellowship, brotherhood, and community between and among all men. Beginning in the Church, therefore, worldly standards must cease to count in relationships among men, or Christ's death and resurrection are mocked. But we in the South have made distinctions of our own creation between men. . . . Thereby, we have contradicted in our faith and life the unity of all men created by God's act in Christ: we have proclaimed the order of the world instead of the Kingdom of Christ; we have crucified Christ anew; we have led the Church to become like the nations, instead of being a light to the nations. But "when anyone is united in Christ, there is a new world. . . . From first to last this has been the work of God." He has reconciled all men to himself and he has entrusted to us the service of reconciliation. We proclaim in faith and with our lives that Christ's reconciliation of all men is neither social stratagem nor political expedient, but the gift of God that has and does and will liberate men from bondage and death—forever more, but also while still in life.

The churches cannot save themselves through good works in race relations; the suggestion is rather that a true church, by definition, makes no room for race. If the church is the last institution to desegregate, Campbell's critics may be forced to wonder if there was not some point in the preaching of this somewhat enigmatic man from Mississippi. ☐

The Post-Assassination Church
By Stephen C. Rose

THE Dean of a great cathedral in the Nation's Capitol rose to preach on the Sunday following President John F. Kennedy's assassination in 1963. His text was from the Prophet Jeremiah. Part of his sermon: "The weapon that killed John Kennedy was not only in the hand of his murderer, but was in the heart of any of us who ever hated, who ever set brother against brother by his selfish spirit. Surely we all do repent that shallow and divisive contentiousness which bred an atmosphere in which some ignorant sharpshooter would one day execute our careless threats. . . . Blame not the man, nor the city, nor the region where the deed was done. But let us search our own hearts to see if pettiness or hostility or unworthy anger did not set the stage for the unworthy act."

Ten days later, Dean Francis B. Sayre, Jr., grandson of a President, perused an editorial in a North Carolina newspaper condemning him for suggesting that the ignoble act of one man might symbolize the corporate guilt of a nation—a guilt, says another Washington pastor, that has dwelt submerged in the American psyche since Hiroshima and Nagasaki, augmented by such sordid events as the aimless death of six Birmingham children and the shot in the back that killed Medgar Evers.

Here surely is the first element of the debate. Does the Biblical Word apply only to the private life of the lone individual, or to the public acts of groups? Does the Word of God speak to staunch churchgoer Billie Sol Estes' personal morality and not to his corporate chicaneries which involved the collusion of other men? Does the Gospel see evil in terms of individual acts in the private realm and not in terms of corporate acts affecting the general public—such as price fixing, quiz-show rigging, or the refusal of a school board to declare an anti-segregation policy? Item number one: The Gospel—public, private, or both?

In August, 1963, the conservative Protestant magazine, *Christianity Today*, reported the following remark made by former Chancellor Conrad Adenauer to the then Vice President Lyndon Johnson: "I have never seen as great a lack of moral integrity as I have among your young people. I do not believe that in the conflict between East and West the young people of the free world have the moral integrity to win." On the basis of this remark, *Christianity Today* offered an analysis that has unquestionable appeal to a great segment of American Protestants: "We believe part of the blame rests squarely on the Church. In recent years the Church has become increasingly concerned with economic, social, and political problems. There has been a corresponding decline in her spiritual mission. As a result people have lost any sense of sin as an offense against a holy God. The churches pay a number of lobbyists in Washington today to work for social and other legislation. . . . Some consider government an agent of the Church. Such folly leads us deeper and deeper into the morass of futility. How can a new society be brought about without new men? . . . The question of the Phillipian jailor still takes priority today: 'Sirs, what must I do to be saved?' And Paul's answer should be the message of the Church in this sophisticated nuclear age: 'Believe on the Lord Jesus Christ, and thou shalt be saved.'"

One cannot help wondering whether the editors of *Christianity Today* would approve of the civil disobedience which resulted in Paul's residence in the Phillipian jail. More serious, however, is the question of what the churches' "spiritual mission" really is. There is complete agreement among all sections of Protestantism that the Church should be more than a social work agency, but there is haziness regarding what the Church has to say. Many are repulsed by the notion that one is "saved" by professing belief in Christ without any commitment to social justice. There are many who doubt that the old-time-religion salvation experience produces "new men."

If one accepts the prescription of *Christianity Today*, what is the Church—a secure club of persons who are "right with God" and therefore absolved from any responsibility in the "heathen world"? A community of persons who see their obligation as one of devotion to Christ and one another, but not to the neighborhood, the world of work, the causes of justice? And yet if one rejects the idea that one is "saved" by merely professing belief, what does one put in its place? The responsible fundamentalists seemed to be saying that God's relationship to the world is fixed, static, immobile. Is not the alternative to suggest that God is always acting in history, that the sense of salvation comes only when one relates to God in a meaningful way in the events of history? Can't one argue that the God of the Old Testament did not retire with the birth of His Son, that His passionate concern with the life of men and nations continues today? And if these things are so, the relationship of the Church to the world should be altered from generation to generation, in response to the dynamic will of God and the changing nature of human need. Here is the second element in the debate: The Church—a group of believers as an end in itself *or* a servant body in a changing world?

The stage for debate is set: In an era of change, what kind of Church? In a world of personal and social disease, what character of ministry? In a period when diffused energies only perpetuate and deepen confusion and decay, what are the vital thrusts, the positive programs, the crucial understandings?

The emerging debate centers on the nature of the Church, and of the individual congregation within the Church. The reason for debate is that the working out of a positive Church program in this decade will threaten the existence of established structures. What emerges should thus be the product of a willingness of all concerned to openly and honestly evaluate every aspect of church life, looking toward renewal.

Surely the first mark of renewal must be the recovery of a sense of authenticity that can be communicated both in public worship and in the activity of the laity both in and beyond the church building. Such renewal can occur only with a different concept of the ministry and of church organization.

One man whose presuppositions are representative of much of the Protestant community is Dean Sayre of the Washington Cathedral. "Our difficulty," he says, "lies in our self-image of what a church is." An essential element in renewal, according to Dean Sayre, is a radical redefinition of what a clergyman should be.

Because the real work of the Church should be carried out in the world, the job of the minister is to be "an assistant or chaplain to the people of the world." Raising his voice, Dean Sayre asks, "Why do we take it for granted that the clergy should run the structures of the Church?" In the first place, if the work of the Church is basically the work of Her people in the world, there is little need for the plethora of activity that now goes on in most churches. And, insofar as the maintenance of the institutional church is a matter of administration for which the clergy are ill-prepared, why shouldn't church administration be turned over to laymen who are experts in such matters?

Perhaps a practical working out of Dean Sayre's suggestion would be for a congregation with more than one minister to hire a layman to handle administration and organizational matters, freeing the clergyman to visit people on their jobs and in their homes, to begin discussions with community leaders, and to devote major time to the job of listening and preaching. An extension of this thought would involve elimination of all congregational activities that duplicate activities of other social institutions, understanding that the layman does not enter the church building to do busy work, but to gain sustenance and direction as he or she seeks to be effective on the job or in the local community.

Once the minister is freed from the suffocating tasks of administration (for which he was never trained), Dean Sayre offers an important warning. The first job of the minister who seeks to become involved with his people is "to listen and learn." If a clergyman is really willing to listen and learn, people will open their doors to him. In short, the clergyman must become "one-half layman." And when the time comes to preach, the function of the preacher is "to deepen the questions . . . to point out the divine dimension of life where it is being lived." The minister whose whole existence is wrapped up in the cocoon of institutional demands will be a deadly preacher, unfamiliar with the world's problems and the problems of his people. When laymen insist that their minister carry a great load of institutional obligations, they only insure his irrelevance.

If the church streamlines its organizations and takes the penetration of existing social structures seriously, what brings the members together? Dean Sayre points to the Sacrament of Holy Communion as the tangible symbol of what Christians share in common: the common cause of suffering with God at the junctions of the world's perpetual need. As the picket line is the tangible sign of common involvement to some participants in the civil rights struggle, so Holy Communion is the token of the Christian's common cause. It is the meeting place of man's need and God's help and, according to Dean Sayre, renewal of the churches involves "developing a liturgy of that help."

Dean Sayre also believes that we must develop new understandings in the theological realm. "The secular world does not believe in the God we've defined. We've left a stupid, frozen, dead impression of God." He adds, as if to place responsibility on those who preach rather than those who seek for faith and meaning, "I don't think we have an atheistic culture, even in Russia."

The situation of world Christianity today seems described by the prophet Ezekiel's vision of the valley of the dry bones. The world thirsts for the decisive Word. Can this be the significance of the tremendous affection and esteem that centered about the late Pope John who was less a symbol of Catholicism than of religion cutting through layers of ecclesiastical inessentials to the very heart of humanity?

The first mark of renewal will certainly involve the freeing of the trained minister to expose himself to the world's problems that he might bring to those problems the light of his training. This will be impossible as long as the minister is burdened with the countless little tasks that go with the maintenance and care of the church's building and institutional life. Perhaps in 1966 the National Council of Churches—representing Christian consensus—will be as definite on this issue as it was on the issue of race in 1963.

Anyone who has sought to move the ecclesiastical monolith —the denominational dinosaur—is painfully aware of the Church's tendency to be "behind the times" in many areas of witness. This is not because the churches have failed to pour funds (however small) into programs designed to provide insight into the great ethical issues. Again the problem is more related to structure and emphasis, not to mention leadership. The high positions in the denominations are reserved for the men concerned with oiling the nuts and bolts of the ecclesiastical enterprise. Commissions on world peace, education, and race tend to be given the back seat.

There is growing evidence that many are becoming discontented with the passive posture of the churches. In many areas of the country contributions to the Church are down. The lull is blamed on the Church's recent participation in the area of race relations, possibly, too, the ardor with which many churchmen supported the candidacy of President Johnson in 1964. But some religious organizations have found that a more relevant posture on the great issues opens up new sources of revenue from laymen who have withheld contributions in the past to a Church which they regarded as peripheral and uninvolved. Denominational executives who are wringing their hands over losses in contributions might consider this point: the less popular the churches become, the less likely chance there is of mass appeal. On the other hand, there is a far greater possibility of genuine commitment that will be reflected in the giving of the concerned.

It is encouraging to note that churches, as they break the cocoon of irrelevance, tend to find effective structures of action. The pressure of the racial crisis forced the National Council of Churches to set up its highly mobile and well-led Commission on Religion and Race. The insidious attempt of radical-rightist groups to intimidate socially concerned suburban congregations will doubtless force ministers and laymen in suburbia to unite for effective rebuttal.

But the great issues remain and there is the feeling that many of them are beyond the reach of the churches, or even, indeed, the myriad voluntary organizations that are set up to deal with a whole gamut of problems. In Chicago, for example, groups that have been working for decades on education often express the feeling that their labors are in vain—the decisions, they surmise, will be dominated by a small "power elite" which they can neither reach directly nor influence from the outside. Fledgling political organizations have sprung up to support everything from municipal reform to world disarmament, but too often they become discouraged by perpetual defeat at the polls.

In addition, one must consider the stiff criteria of an organization that might inspire people to join, give, and sacrifice. It should be an organization with goals specific enough to be understood and worked for by the constituency. The organization should have enough structure to insure the employment of each member's talent where it will do the most good. (The socially concerned doctor whose main church job is Sunday morning ushering is a good example of the misuse of talent). The organization should be willing to give up functions that can be better carried out by another group, both to avoid duplication and increase effectiveness. The organization should set certain disciplines as a membership requirement, at the same time having a democratic government that gives representation to the views of all the membership. The organization should have built-in mechanisms for action and evaluation. How many churches give consideration to such criteria, even as they meet in seemingly endless sessions to decide, "What is our mission?"

Let me suggest further the sorts of activity that organizations of the concerned might schedule. Activity should be geared to crucial issues, whether they are the dramatic issues of race and world peace, or the less romantic areas of caring for the elderly, helping troubled youth or maintaining a community. Then the group should decide what approach it is able to make on selected issues. If the group is small it will be best to isolate a single issue which it has the power to do something about. For our purposes we can suggest three types of voluntary groups: the study-recommendation group; the direct service group; and the direct action group.

The study-recommendation group builds on the well-known study group concept. Ordinarily such groups meet to discuss a problem without any built-in plan of action. They propose grandiose schemes in their study sessions, but the very nature of the groups renders such planning irrelevant. Such a group must recognize from the outset the limited possibility of any action other than a recommendation, either to the powers that be, or if that fails to an appropriate group (perhaps itself) that will be structured for direct service or direct action.

The scope of the study-recommendation group seems small, but it is much more satisfying to function well with a small mandate than to flounder hopelessly in a sea of undefined possibilities.

The direct service group is already aware of a need that it feels it can meet. It is constituted with the necessary manpower and talent to meet that need, and that need only. The need may be as prosaic as the desire of new residents to be introduced to their local community. Or it may be a communications setup to insure the maximum enforcement of fair housing in a neighborhood. The important thing is that the group is taking on something it can handle and is acting directly on that problem. There is no reason why the Church cannot spawn such direct service groups. The tendency is to flounder too long in the study area. Direct service should not be confused with direct action: it is geared solely to service of a certain type. It seeks volunteers only to meet the specific need. The direct service offered will not be self-consciously controversial. Its purpose will not be to arouse a community, though this may be an incidental aspect. The Freedom Schools in Mississippi, the efforts of certain groups to provide birth control information, and the maintenance of open housing are all examples of direct service projects that have had to face persecution because of their unpopularity.

But it is neither necessary nor specifically Christian that such service groups always be controversial. Some—like church related coffee houses, counselling clinics, and tutoring programs—will be quiet exemplars of the call to witness in the undramatic but crucial corners of our perpetual need. And no amount of Puritan prudery will erase the fact that the Church is called to minister to joy as well as sorrow.

The direct action group, as defined here, is specifically oriented toward the great power structures. Its purpose is to influence these structures for the good of humanity. No area is more touchy. And no area is more complex. But it is precisely the sense of impotence in the face of the great power structures—government, the law, big business, big unions—that gives rise to a general sense of apathy. The slogan, "You can't fight city hall," is feeding the frustrations of many in our society and the problem is not just city hall.

The complexity arises from such questions as these: How does one become involved in the decision-making which will guide the War on Poverty? How does one affect such seemingly obscure but ultimately important issues as urban zoning, fair and just taxation, unemployment, disarmament? How does one locate the real power structure—whether it be the Federal government, state or local authority, the big corporation or the union? Direct action groups may sometimes find a home within existing political parties and representative structures, but often there is no chance of significant influence through traditional channels. Then too, impatience with the status quo may lead a direct action group to do all it can to fight the power structures for purposes of publicity and thus of ultimate strategy.

Direct action may very well involve demonstrations, picketing, symbolic gestures including such extreme acts as self-immolation in South Vietnam. It will be misunderstood, vilified and discounted until crisis dictates compromise. And one can never defend direct action in general terms—always one must weigh the specifics to see whether the objectives sought are more likely to be gained by other means. Of course nonviolence plays a part in any consideration of direct action. Americans can be grateful that the strong leadership of men like Martin Luther King has stemmed the possibility of even more tragic incidents than have already occurred.

How is the Church to foster responsible, effective direct action? The first necessity will be to attach to every important decision-making body in our society a competent person whose job is to call in cadres of experienced Churchmen to testify on relevant bills, influence important industrial and union decisions, and generally keep tabs on the decision-making bodies. There are many areas where lack of agreement among Church members makes such a program difficult. But can there be more than occasional disagreement on the following issues?

—fair housing.
—penal reform.
—the need for a reduction of air pollution.
—the need for humane city planning.
—disarmament.
—humane laws insuring the rights of migrant workers.
—viable programs to share America's food surplus with the world's starving millions.
—adequate education.
—imaginative television and radio.
—the need for a more vigilant and crusading press.
—destruction of all barriers to equal opportunity.

We give assent to such goals in multitudes of meetings, but the churches have yet to take the most minimal steps to insure that their vast resources will be turned upon the problem of bringing about decisions within the power structures. The blood brother of apathy is the inability to give priority to what is important.

It is my conviction that our age is not one of "a failure of nerve," a "stifling of imagination," or any of the many hopeless epithets of those who make a living by selling pessimistic diagnoses of everything under the sun. We are not about to embark on a primrose path to a great society in which man will deserve deification in a pantheon of tin gods. But we have been given the opportunity in history to organize our enthusiasms more effectively than we are doing today.

If the churches will not do the job, there will be defections of those who desire not to assert their superiority but merely to get on with the task at hand. But the continued structural inadequacies of the churches will be a great liability. The failure to loose imaginative young men and women on a host of exploratory programs will result in a greater decline of influence than we know today. Words alone will no longer suffice, for we have heard the call to arms at one hundred religious gatherings. Structural reorganization and a rearrangement of priorities is now the only medicine for the dying denominations. And even if such painful self-evaluation and change results in institutional death, there will be a more significant rebirth than would result from death-by-default.

What follows is motivated, in part, by a desire to escape the charge so often aimed at critics of the present day church: the charge that such criticism is never accompanied by constructive suggestion. Certainly we should be encouraged by the visible evidences of renewal in our own time: the slow but positive road to ecumenical cooperation, the growth of serious study in the churches, and the occasional but rewarding ventures of the churches into areas of real service. Likewise we should note that the general decline of preaching has not prevented the emergence of a reliable band of "preachers" (many not in the parish) who are confronting us with the message of God's reality. The most important positive factor is the apparent willingness of many within Protestantism to consider new forms of the church and to seek new depth in Christian life. It is with this in mind that the following suggestions are offered.

THE LOCAL CHURCH. In the context of the need to streamline the local church program and free the minister from the burden of administration, the following steps might be taken:

- Churches with multiple staffs should hire laymen to handle administrative tasks such as fund-raising, building maintenance, etc. When an individual congregation cannot afford this, such services should be obtained cooperatively with other churches. Ministers should be free to do what they were trained to do: prepare sermons, make pastoral calls, and become "chaplains to the laity."

- Unless absolutely necessary, church construction should be limited to cooperative ventures on the part of several churches. There is no good reason why Christian education in a given community cannot take place in a central facility available to all Protestant groups. Duplication of facilities wastes time, money, and effort. Directors of Christian education hired by several churches should pool their resources to form a cooperative faculty, conducting classes throughout the week rather than confining the main emphasis to the often awkward Sunday School hour. Whenever possible, curriculum for Christian education should be developed on the local level so that national denominations can begin to cut down on the enormous expense of producing materials that are often useless at the local level.

- The entire organization of church music needs overhauling. Many churches can't support an adequate choir and those that can tend to make music their God. When possible communities should support a single choir which would be available to churches on a revolving basis. In many churches the perpetuation of the choir is a waste of manpower, and the tendency of many choirs is to remove singing from the congregation, where it rightfully belongs. New churches should think twice before replacing their electric organs with expensive pipe organs: they sound nice, but the pursuit of justice might be a better use of funds. In many communities there is a church with an exceptional music program. Such churches should undertake to fulfill the legitimate need of the total community for high-quality music, cutting down on duplication of effort.

- Most lay activities within the church should be carefully reevaluated and redirected. Service to the community should be the criterion and there should be absolutely no barriers to service, once needs are determined. If the major community problem is divorce, let the local church meet that problem, perhaps using the church building as a marriage-counselling clinic. The church building should be open to the community at all times. In communities where people are lonely and in need of friendship, perhaps the greatest service the local congregation can render is to keep the doors open and the coffee pot on, providing a place where people feel free to come, sit, talk, meet others. Groups like Gamblers Anonymous, Alcoholics Anonymous, peace movements, and other worthwhile efforts should be free to use the church's physical plants.

• Local congregations should conduct an ongoing study of denominational programs and expenses, and adjust their contributions to denominations on bases like the following: How much money is going into service? Is the denomination trying to work cooperatively with other denominations? It may be that local programs, in which laymen are actively involved, are more worthy of direct support.

• When a congregation is aware of a need that is not being met by other organizations, it should mobilize, cooperatively when possible, to meet that need. If the need is for community counselling, youth work, or political action in the cause of justice, it may be that specialized techniques and personnel will be required. It is expected that laymen will be equipped to devise means of effective service. Once a group of laymen and laywomen has decided to tackle a problem, the persons involved should be freed from other major responsibilities within the congregation in order to have as much time as possible to realize the potential mission.

• Fund-raising should be limited to a single annual appeal, preferably a pledge system. Special offerings should be limited or eliminated, and all fund-raising activities of church organizations should be drastically curtailed: fairs, bazaars, bake sales, etc.

• The local church should not regard Sunday morning as the only time during the week for public worship. Hours of public worship should be determined by the needs of the community. All Protestant churches should offer Holy Communion on a weekly basis or perhaps twice weekly so that all members may have the opportunity to share the sacrament.

• Churches should reevaluate the meaning of membership, requiring in-depth training for new members and courses for old members who have not had training. Basic education for membership should include an introduction to the Old and New Testament, a course in church history, a course in contemporary social problems from the Christian perspective, and special-interest courses designed to equip members for service in the world. It is possible that churches might require a basic commitment of five percent of gross family income annually as a pledge to support the institution, thus eliminating the tremendous time and expense of the church's far-flung fund raising efforts. The Biblical tithe is ten percent, but in our world when the church is no longer the major custodian of the public welfare, the other five percent might be applied to additional charitable and service enterprises.

- The Protestant church—on an interdenominational basis —should set uniform standards of training for the clergyman as counsellor, offering some sort of public recognition to the minister who is so trained. Such a program might aid in the creation of badly needed pastoral counselling clinics throughout the country. In some communities such clinics might be set up on a cooperative basis.

It is unlikely that local congregations will have the funds or flexibility to engage in many of the creative ministries that are needed if the churches are to renew their life. Denominations, acting locally and nationally, should be the catalyst for a number of creative programs that need immediate consideration. In order to act in such a manner, a drastic curtailment of much present denominational activity is necessary. The following items suggest such revisions in denominational programming.

- Denominations could make drastic reductions in funds spent on all manner of publishing ventures which are presently repetitious and often a waste of the churchgoer's money. It would be most interesting to know the amount of money denominations spend to raise money. Denominational publications could be simplified and in some cases eliminated in favor of cooperative magazines, etc. There should also be an impartial evaluation of the validity of spending large sums on national radio-television ministries. It might be better for Protestants to pool resources to produce one or two programs at prime-time hours on television rather than a large number of programs which are seen in the early Sunday morning hours when most people are asleep. It is interesting to note that where Protestants are more involved in service than in publicizing themselves, the networks are quick to seize the chance to produce challenging documentaries which cost denominations nothing and are usually eminently creative.

- In line with a decreased emphasis on church construction (often a product of denominational competition of the most hypocritical and dishonest variety), the amount of money reserved for this doubtful activity should be used for mission pursuits: the establishing of forms and structures appropriate to the modern era. Some denominational executives argue that the only "successful" church is a growing one, an assertion which has been demonstrated to be untrue in countless cases of significant Christian action by small, dedicated groups. The numbers game is more appropriate to the large corporation than to the churches. Incidentally one of the biggest barriers to denominational relevance is the way in which denominations are chopped up into separate and often quite autonomous departments. The Social Action people live in one wing of the building, unable to effect the policies of the Stewardship Department, while the Church Extension executives have a field day without the consultation of the Home Missions officials. Unity in mission? Not by a long shot. Self-interest and self-perpetuation? In many cases this constitutes the greatest barrier to denominational mission, and the barrier is erected behind the backs of laymen.

- Denominations should pool their resources into a giant, national contingency fund for the creation of relevant ministries. If a competent individual needs money to implement an idea, he should be able to look to the church for backing, both financial and spiritual. It is sad but true that many of today's more creative ministries are supported not by churches, but by private foundations who are more broad in their scope of interest.

There are countless additional proposals that might help pave the way for the renewal of Protestantism. One suggestion, made by a Chicago religion editor, is that the National Council of Churches might gather the churches together into a sort of Protestant Vatican Council—a meeting which would last as long as might be necessary to hammer out various reforms within Protestantism. The notion of a Protestant Ecumenical Council has considerable merit and should be investigated. At present the National Council of Churches meets every three years, with limited representation, and then only for a week at a time. Such a Council might be convened cooperatively with evangelical and fundamentalist branches of Protestantism in order to seek a healing of a gap that has existed ever since Darwin published his Bible-disturbing theory of evolution.

It is possible that adult education within the churches could be accomplished more efficiently if groups of ministers and lay teachers were assigned to cover whole communities, conducting programs in many churches. In Chicago such a program is being carried out by the Ecumenical Institute.

One of the most serious matters facing the churches—and facing them now—is the growing difficulty in finding young persons of insight and ability who are willing to enter the ministry. A faculty member at one of the country's prominent seminaries estimates that for many students the Peace Corps has more attraction than the ministry. Could this be because the Peace Corps offers opportunity for direct service and full commitment without the red tape and uncertainty that tends to surround the life of the minister? Until the churches free sufficient funds to allow for the working of the creative visions of a new generation of laymen and ministers, the chances for a rapid decline in theological enrollment and an increased number of ministers deciding to leave their professions are so certain as to threaten the very foundation of the present order.

Seminaries should take the lead in determining what types of ministry students would like to create if they were completely free to choose. Many ideas would emerge: industrial missions, mobile ministries in leisure time areas, chaplaincies to specific groups within our society, the establishment of rehabilitation centers for ex-prisoners, the formation of house churches, the creation of an Ecumenical Peace Corps to work in depressed areas of this country. Such programs are already being initiated, but they are done on such a small scale that it is very difficult for an able young minister to find immediate employ in his area of interest.

At present the entire economic life of the churches is based on the dubious enterprise of church extension. Build more churches, get more members. *Ergo:* increased contributions. The emphasis is on expansion, often at the price of depth of commitment or membership standards. Average giving to churches in such a situation is only a fraction of what it should be, and for good reason. Members are largely uninvolved in a creative program in which their money seems to make a real difference. If the church is to be a servant in the world, it will seek fewer members and more depth.

Until the denominations are willing to risk a decline in contributions in order to pursue a positive program of renewal, it is doubtful that the relevance of the Protestant church will increase. In fact it is probable that popular apathy with today's *status quo* will result in a decline in membership anyway. If the church is to decrease in size, it might at least do so honorably. The religious revival of the past decade is over; it is now time for renewal.

It may sound strange to say so, but perhaps the general failure of the churches can be related to a symptom if not a cause: Biblical illiteracy, most particularly illiteracy in relation to the Old Testament.

If the following questions all evoke a negative response, there is certainly room for remedial action. Does the Old Testament play a significant role in the public worship of your congregation? Is it the basis for sermons? Is the Old Testament studied? Is it possible to understand the New Testament without reference to the Old?

The Old Testament is of fundamental importance for the following reasons:

—The Old Testament was the "Bible" of the early Church.

—The Old Testament understands God not as some abstract idea, but as the One who is active in history, the One who loves, judges, redeems, comforts . . . always in specific situations, always in history.

—The Old Testament is essentially a story of God's activity in the world, from the creation through the long and painful history of Israel, leading up to the birth of Christ. Without reference to this story, the New Testament is like the final scene of Hamlet torn from the context of the first five acts. Without reference to the Old Testament, the Christian Gospel is utterly incomprehensible. Christ's coming was the supreme development in God's relationship to the world, but why did He come? See the Old Testament.

—The Old Testament understands the *corporate* nature of life. God is seen dealing with entire nations. The social ills of whole societies are portrayed with contemporary relevance in the writings of the Prophets. How are we to comprehend the present racial crisis without reference to the Old Testament? God is patient. He gives warnings and signs to mankind. But then, in the face of perpetual rebellion, he acts! He passes judgment and the judgment (that equality will come, that the poor nations will be granted their due, that the complacent country decays) is worked out within history's fabric.

—In the Old Testament Israel is granted a special relationship to God. Israel is His messenger in the world. The best contemporary definition of the Church is that, through Christ, the Church is the New Israel. Because Israel is close to God, the relationship is turbulent. God will not let Israel (the Church) go, but He will chastise her and turn his back in anger when Israel becomes complacent.

—The Christian Gospel speaks of being free from the Law. How is the Christian to know that from which he is freed without reference to the Law? Where is the law which God requires of man? In the Old Testament.

—The Christian faith has remained incomprehensible to intellectuals largely because Christian thinkers have tried to make the dynamic nature of God—revealed in the Old Testament—fit the abstract, formal principles and disciplines of classical philosophy. The Old Testament, the Bible as a whole, provides an angle of vision that can never be fully described by philosophy.

The Old Testament is an exciting book. It could give impetus to preaching. It could open the eyes of laymen. Today it seems to be the Forgotten Testament.

It would be pleasant to end on a dogmatic note, summing everything up in ten contemporary commandments: END SEGREGATION! STOP PANDERING SELF-INTEREST DISGUISED AS PATRIOTISM! DO NOT COMMIT ADULTERY! DO NOT KILL, OR CONTRIBUTE TO DEATH BY SUPPORTING THE INSTITUTIONS OF WAR! BE HONEST! BE CREATIVE! STOP JUDGING OTHERS! LOVE YOUR ENEMIES! STOP ACTING AS IF THE

WORLD RESTED ON YOUR SHOULDERS! CEASE BOWING DOWN AT THE ALTARS OF FALSE GODS! The difficulty Americans have in keeping such commandments should be enough to give pause to the person who is optimistic about human nature. But even when men and women are actively engaged in attempting to eliminate the evils of war, family disintegration, and selfish interest on the part of every major group in our society, the possibility of progress is uncertain. Problems grow in complexity and answers are easy to state but hard to implement.

The major progress that the Protestant churches will make depends on a slow change of emphasis rather than on the swift implementation of some new program. Someday it will become apparent that the churches are not social clubs or real-estate operations. Someday the prodding of a God who acts and judges will force current unsolved problems into the open: automation, true integration, population, a creative approach to the relationship of government to the individual, equal education—a host of others. One can cajole, ridicule, warn—and still we shall remain lukewarm. It is easier for us to erect monuments and rename expressways and light eternal flames (in order to avoid commitment ourselves) than it is for us to change. And it is naive to expect the churches to accept even the changes that are obviously designed to increase effectiveness. There are big if's ahead for Protestantism. They are related to the question of whether basic, entrenched attitudes can be changed. There will always be small pockets of obedience within society; often the legitimate mission of the churches has been taken over by persons who have left the church in rebellion because of the church's slowness and insensitivity. Thus one need not rest all of his hope upon the chance that major reforms will take place on the congregational and denominational level. Chances are they may not. The point is that it would be nice if they did. □

A NOTE ON THE CONTRIBUTORS:

in order of appearance

ROBERT STROM is an ordained Presbyterian minister. Currently he is on the staff of the West Side Organization, Chicago, an alliance of unemployed persons seeking to bring about constructive changes in the public welfare system.

PEGGY WAY is Program Director of the Chicago City Missionary Society. An ordained minister, she was instrumental in forming the Volunteer Training Program which prepares laymen for specialized service in the inner city.

DR. L. K. BISHOP is the former Executive Director of People to People, an agency devoted to the maintenance of good international relations through direct person-to-person encounters. He is now Vice President of the Chicago College of Osteopathy.

DON BENEDICT is the Executive Director of the Chicago City Missionary Society. A pioneer in the Protestant inner city movement, he was instrumental in the organization of parishes in New York and Cleveland. In his present post, he is responsible for the supervision of more than twenty experimental and direct-service ministries in Chicago.

BRUCE HUNT is on the staff of the Chicago Business Industrial Project, an experimental program sponsored by the Chicago City Missionary Society and by interested laymen.

GORDON COSBY is one of the founders and the minister of the Church of the Saviour, Washington, D. C.

JOHN FRY is the former News Editor of *Presbyterian Life*. He is presently the minister of the First Presbyterian Church, Chicago, Ill.

JARED RARDIN is a graduate of Union Theological Seminary who has served at the Church of the Saviour, Washington, D. C. He is presently one of the ministers of First Methodist Church, Germantown, Pa.

HOWARD MOODY is minister of the Judson Memorial Church, New York City. He has been active in New York politics and is a member of the World Council of Church's study committee on the missionary structure of the congregation.

ROBERT SPIKE has served with distinction as Executive Director of the National Council of Church's Commission on Religion and Race. He is presently a Professor of Ministry at the Divinity School, the University of Chicago.

BILL SOUTHWICK is the director of The Door, an experimental coffee house in Chicago sponsored by the North Side Cooperative Ministry.

HARVEY COX is a member of the theological faculty of the Harvard Divinity School. He is the author of *The Secular City* (*Macmillan,* 1965) and a member of the editorial boards of *Renewal* and *Christianity and Crisis.*

A NOTE ON THE EDITOR:

STEPHEN C. ROSE is Editor of Renewal Magazine. He is a graduate of Exeter, Williams College and Union Theological Seminary. In 1961 he served as part of the Student Interracial Ministry Project in Nashville, Tenn. He is a member of the editorial board of *Christianity and Crisis* and has written the narration for two films, *The City of Necessity* and *Eden, U.S.A.* He lives in Chicago with his wife and two children.

A NOTE ON RENEWAL MAGAZINE:

With one exception all of the articles in this book appeared originally in *Renewal Magazine. Renewal* is sponsored jointly by the Chicago City Missionary Society and the New York City Mission Society. It has a national circulation of 30,000 and in 1965 was the recipient of a citation from the Associated Church Press for "editorial courage through creative and crusading content." *Renewal* is concerned primarily with the Church and the emerging metropolis. Through single-theme issues on subjects ranging from urban poverty and civil rights to the financial posture of the Churches, *Renewal* seeks to awaken those inside and outside the churches to the challenges of our time. Each issue of the magazine is, in a sense, a small book, complete with superb photographs in the best tradition of social journalism. Recent issues include "Youth Today: Pests or Prophets?"—an examination of a new generation in America whose leaders express themselves in song (Bob Dylan) and in painstaking grass-roots organizing in urban ghettoes (Tom Hayden); "What Price Relevance?"—an inquiry into the spending practices of American Protestant churches; and "Apathy in The Metropolis"—a report in depth on the emergence of apathy as the number one disease of modern urban life. *Renewal* maintains contact with the most exciting experiments within the Church and with the trouble spots in society. Because of both format and timely subject matter *Renewal* has become an important adult education resource in churches throughout the United States.

Additional copies of this book may be ordered from your local bookstore or by writing directly to Renewal Magazine, 19 South La Salle Street, Chicago, Illinois 60603. Information regarding subscriptions to Renewal Magazine may be obtained at the same address.